the backpacker's handbook

Backpacking in Rocky Mountain National Park.
(National Park Service Photo; Fred E. Mang, Jr.)

the backpacker's handbook

by george sullivan

GROSSET & DUNLAP
A National General Company
Publishers   New York

Library of Congress Catalog No.: 73-183025
ISBN: 0-448-01214-6 (Hardbound)
ISBN: 0-448-01872-1 (Paperbound)

Printed in the United States of America

Acknowledgment

Special thanks are offered to Burton V. Coale, Regional Chief, Public Affairs, Midwest Region, National Park Service, for making available the many excellent photographs depicting backcountry hiking and camping in Rocky Mountain National Park.

Contents

the backpacker's handbook

Introduction

The backpacker is very much an individualist. He voluntarily cuts himself off from society, becoming almost entirely self-dependent. He conducts himself as he wants to, not as traditional modes of behavior prescribe or as the establishment dictates.

The opportunity to assert one's individuality is surely one of the chief reasons that backpacking has become so popular. There are others. According to research conducted recently by Dr. Daniel Henning at Eastern Montana College, a prime benefit of the backcountry, the wilderness, is stress removal. A Philadelphia school teacher told Dr. Henning, "I feel as though I'm in another world, completely divorced from the cares of the other. I forget all my personal and professional problems." American conservationist and naturalist John Muir recognized this benefit a century ago, when he described "the great fresh, unblighted, unredeemed wilderness . . ." as a place where ". . . the galling harness of civilization drops off, and the wounds heal ere we are aware."

Personal achievement is another reason people backpack. A college girl told Dr. Henning, ". . . who would have ever thought that I could hike fifteen miles in a day with a knapsack on my back?"

Whatever your own motive, this guidebook should help. It appraises backpacking equipment of all types. It explains the technical side of hiking and camping overnight. It tells what foods to buy and how to prepare them. It surveys where to backpack. In a phrase, it's meant to get you off on the right foot.

A supervised group trip is best for your first ventures into the back-country.
(U.S.D.A. Forest Service; Jim Hughes)

CHAPTER ONE
Preparing

Backpacking makes special physical demands on any individual. If you have never tented out or done much hiking outside of city parks, you will need some grooming for anything more than an overnight trip.

As a starter, try a hike that lasts only a few hours. Wear jeans and any lightweight, comfortable shoes. Take your lunch and a container of water.

Overnight hikes come next. Now you'll need bedding, perhaps shelter (depending on where you're going to be traveling and the time of year) and a variety of accessory items (listed in Chapters Two, Three and Seven). Plan carefully. Select a short, easy route. Plan meals that aren't going to present any problems.

Hiking and Camping Organizations

There are dozens of organizations that can be helpful to you at this stage. Not only will they provide you with up-to-date information on hiking and camping activities in your area, but most of them sponsor group trips. Traveling with experienced backpackers is the best way to gain the knowledge and skills you require.

Virtually all hiking and camping organizations are listed in the appendix, along with the address for each. The most important national and regional ones are described below.

For backpackers in the eastern sector of the United States, there is the Appalachian Trail Conference which is composed of thirty-three hiking clubs who maintain and support the 2,050 miles of the Maine-to-Georgia Appalachian Trail, the longest continuously marked trail in the world. In addition to the member clubs, there are seventy-five affiliated clubs who support the activities of the Conference. The Conference publishes dozens of booklets and maps relating to the Appalachian Trail and provides up-to-date information on trail conditions throughout the year.

The New York–New Jersey Trail Conference is a federation of hiking clubs in the New York metropolitan area which maintains over 700 miles of trails in northern New Jersey and southeastern New York, including a portion of the Appalachian Trail. It has a combined membership of about 50,000 and publishes informative material which is available to both members and nonmembers. This material includes a long list of guides and maps plus a bimonthly newsletter, *The Trail Walker*. The New England Trail Conference has member clubs throughout much of the northeastern United States. It provides maps of major Eastern trails, guidebooks and informative pamphlets.

The Sierra Club, founded in 1892 by noted American naturalist John Muir "to help people explore, enjoy and protect parks, wildernesses, waters, forests and wildlife," has become an important influence in conservation and environmental affairs, but it also provides many services expressly for hikers and campers. It is a large organization, with 63,000 members, and chapters in eleven states — Arizona, California, Colorado, Illinois, Michigan, Nevada, New Mexico, New York, Oregon, Texas, Washington and Wisconsin and Washington, D.C.

Throughout the year, the Sierra Club organizes hiking trips for backpackers of varying degrees of experience. The simplest is the Base Camp Trip, which is a day's hike into backcountry from a road end. Mules carry equipment and provisions; a cook and commissary crew furnish the meals, and experienced guides conduct hikes and climbs from the base camp.

The Club's Knapsack Trips are a bit more demanding. Groups

Sierra Club chapters (See appendix for addresses).

of twenty carry everything they need with them, and they perform camp chores themselves. Some of these are called Leisure Trips and proceed at an unhurried pace, while others are of cross-country nature and can be rigorous. The Club's High-Light Trip, composed of about fifty people, is the most arduous of all. There are pack mules and a small commissary crew, but each person carries a pack of up to twenty pounds. The party covers ten to fourteen miles a day, and the going can be rough. High-Light trips have taken backpackers to the Sawtooth Mountains in Idaho, the Grand Tetons of Wyoming and the Cascades of the Pacific Northwest.

The High Trip is the Sierra Club's standby. Made up of about one hundred people plus a commissary crew, a High Trip covers five to ten miles a day, usually at altitudes of about nine thousand feet, although sometimes as high as eleven thousand or twelve thousand feet. Pack animals carry equipment and each camper's personal gear. Usually there are layovers of two or three days to allow for exploration and the pursuit of nature interests.

The Sierra Club publishes a long list of authoritative books and pamphlets covering many phases of hiking and camping. One of the Club's totebooks, *Food for Knapsackers*, is considered the definitive book on the subject. Write and request a free book list.

As one other of its many services, the Sierra Club sells a three-ounce stainless steel drinking cup for $1. It is rugged, easy to clean and probably one of the most practical utensils you will ever see. Dangling from one's belt, furthermore, it is one of backpacking's most cherished status symbols.

The Wilderness Society is another organization of special importance to western hikers and campers. While it specializes in riding trips into the high country, it also organizes and conducts backpacking trips for those with experience in backcountry travel.

Most young people are familiar with American Youth Hostels, a nonprofit organization with the aim of "encouraging people of

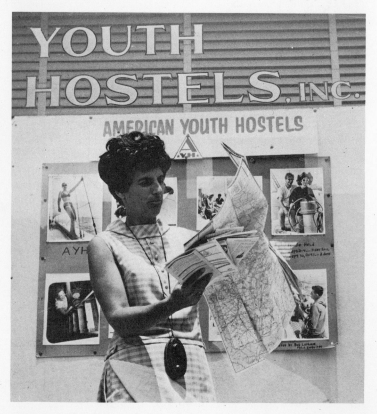

American Youth Hostels helps hikers and campers in finding overnight accommodations.
(American Youth Hostels, Inc.)

all ages to enjoy the out-of-doors . . . and to travel simply and in-expensively, staying in hostels in the United States and forty-six countries abroad."

The term "youth hostels" simply refers to overnight accom-modations in settings that are scenic, historical or cultural. A hostel can be a school, church, modern building or specially built facility. Overnight fees in the United States range from $1.50 to $2.00. There are about one hundred hostels in the United States, and 75,000 people are authorized to use them.

AYH has twenty-seven councils, each of which sponsors out-door activities on a year-round basis, planning day trips or ex-tended treks in the United States, Canada and abroad. Pacific Coast councils offer extensive backpacking and hiking programs as part of their regular event schedule. Councils also organize AYH Clubs, which are smaller hosteling groups. There are about seventy-five of these.

Mazamas is a well-known private mountaineering club that conducts trail trips from a weekend in length to an entire summer, but mountain climbing is what the organization emphasizes. Climbing a snow peak is one qualification of membership.

The outings conducted by the various branches and affiliates of the National Audubon Society — there are almost four hundred of them — are sometimes no more than nature walks, but the organization can be helpful in providing information on local trails and hiking activities.

The National Campers and Hikers Association is much more oriented toward camping than hiking, describing itself as the "oldest, largest and fastest-growing family camping organization in North America." The organization has about five hundred local chapters, and provides members with information on local campsites, roads and trails; it also publishes reports evaluating camping and hiking equipment.

Terrain and Climate

Learn all you possibly can about the terrain and climate of the area that you plan to visit. The best available maps for anyone going into remote sections of the country are the topographical maps prepared by the U.S. Geological Survey. Drawn in elabo-rate detail, they show roads, trails, streams, bridges and every facet of terrain. There is nothing to compare with them.

These maps come in six different scales, from 1:24,000 (meaning that every unit of measurement on the map is represented by 24,000 similar units on the earth's surface) to 1:500,000. With the former, one inch equals about three-eighths of a mile (or 2,000 feet); with the latter, one inch equals about eight miles (or 42,240 feet).

A map with a 1:24,000 scale for the state of Rhode Island would take up an area about the size of Providence, so these maps are issued in what the Geographical Surveys calls quadrangles, either $7\frac{1}{2}°$ or 15° quadrangles (referring to minutes, both latitude and longitude). Each quadrangle costs 60c to 75c.

To secure maps of this type for the area that you plan to travel, write the U.S. Geological Survey (GSA Building, Washington, D.C. 20242) and request an index to the topographical maps of your state or the general area in which you are interested. This will enable you to order the quadrangles that you require.

There are several U.S.G.S. map offices or distribution centers throughout the United States, and any one of these will supply you with the index or the maps you want. The central distribution facility for maps covering areas east of the Mississippi River is: Distribution Section, U.S.G.S., Washington, D.C. 20242. For maps west of the Mississippi, the address is: Distribution Section, U.S.G.S., Federal Center, Denver, Colorado 80225. For Alaska: U.S.G.S., 520 Illinois St., Fairbanks, Alaska. There are also map distribution centers in Dallas, Texas; Salt Lake City, Utah; Spokane, Washington; Menlo Park and San Francisco, California; and Anchorage, Juneau and Palmer, Alaska.

Quadrangle maps are also sold at most National Forest and National Park headquarters (listed in your telephone directory under "United States Government, Interior Department"), or local map retailers (listed in the Yellow Pages under "Maps").

The National Park and National Forest Service also issue maps, sometimes called trail maps. These show marked paths or beaten tracks but not too much else, and hardly approach the U.S.G.S. topographical maps in detail.

Maps for Canada that are comparable to the U.S.G.S. maps are available through the Map Distribution Office of the Department of Mines and Technical Surveys (615 Booth St., Ottawa, Ontario). In your request for information, make reference to maps of the National Topographical Series.

When you obtain your topographical maps, study the contour lines carefully. These are the lines which connect points of equal altitude. They are broken at intervals by figures which indicate

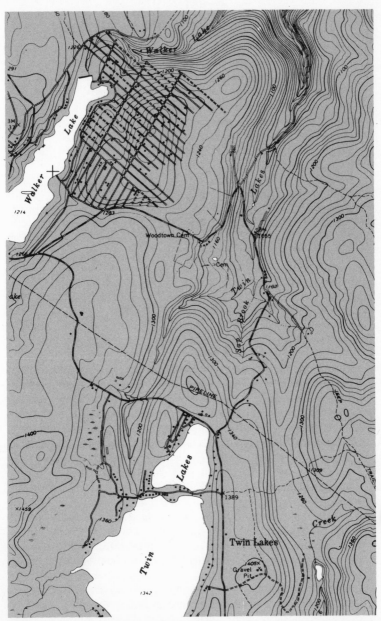

This is part of the Shohola Quadrangle, a tiny section of northeastern Pennsylvania bordering New York state, as mapped by the Geographical Survey. Contour lines are at intervals of twenty feet.

Year	Jan.	Feb.	Mar.	Apr.	May	June	July	Aug.	Sept.	Oct.	Nov.	Dec.	Annual
D	3.13	2.86	3.14	2.47	3.48	3.07	3.89	4.08	2.85	3.24	3.21	2.89	38.31
F	24	24	24	25	25	24	24	24	24	24	24	24	-
1931	2.20	2.74	2.62	4.35	4.69	5.26	4.68	4.79	1.75	1.55	1.95	3.29	39.87
1932	3.95	1.99	5.07	2.59	3.55	3.75	2.29	5.61	1.10	5.59	8.31	1.53	45.33
1933	2.05	3.48	4.86	6.03	1.86	1.17	3.12	8.71	6.18	2.26	.89	3.31	43.92
1934	3.02	2.20	2.95	4.47	4.91	3.34	6.72	2.35	-9.89	2.20	3.13	1.95	47.13
1935	3.32	2.45	1.84	3.08	1.79	3.45	3.56	1.29	2.92	2.35	4.83	1.09	31.97
1936	3.94	2.86	4.99	3.38	2.48	3.38	4.34	6.99	3.13	3.19	1.71	4.66	45.05
1937	6.42	1.86	2.73	4.51	4.08	6.38	2.95	3.91	3.11	2.96	2.92	2.32	44.15
1938	2.95	1.55	1.61	2.06	4.39	5.95	7.08	5.97	9.85	1.83	2.24	2.51	47.99
1939	2.26	3.78	2.75	4.28	1.18	2.48	2.70	2.04	2.24	4.27	1.32	1.22	30.52
1940	.98	2.01	3.66	4.69	5.58	3.33	4.45	3.13	2.64	2.00	4.35	2.88	39.70
1941	2.17	2.22	.95	.78	1.64	4.80	5.01	2.39	.87	1.78	1.92	2.64	27.17
1942	2.76	1.81	4.98	.87	2.79	2.68	4.03	4.37	3.40	3.87	4.54	4.59	40.69
1943	2.67	1.56	2.58	3.14	5.51	4.46	6.47	1.10	1.73	6.67	3.70	.51	40.10
1944	.98	1.33	4.22	3.28	1.79	5.08	3.50	.61	4.87	1.45	4.88	2.98	34.97
1945	4.06	3.50	1.89	4.77	7.49	5.82	10.77	5.73	5.60	2.40	4.41	3.81	60.25
1946	1.14	2.62	1.58	1.50	4.61	2.93	5.97	2.95	3.68	1.42	.76	2.12	31.28
1947	2.53	1.84	2.39	4.30	5.06	4.32	4.36	3.24	2.85	2.43	6.09	3.18	42.59
1948	3.06	1.92	3.12	4.57	4.41	4.34	2.10	2.35	.78	1.99	3.85	7.40	39.86
1949	4.76	2.16	1.03	2.76	5.25	.56	4.73	2.00	2.32	2.77	1.67	3.85	33.86
1950	3.52	3.92	2.50	2.07	3.59	4.36	2.70	3.63	1.74	1.13	3.76	2.80	35.72
1951	1.92	4.58	5.10	2.38	3.19	2.51	-	3.59	-	3.49	5.49	4.47	-
1952	4.20	2.08	3.02	7.57	4.70	4.39	3.85	4.44	5.04	1.01	2.07	3.59	45.96
G	2.95	2.48	3.02	3.52	3.84	3.85	4.54	3.69	3.60	2.66	3.40	3.03	40.58
H	22	22	22	22	22	22	21	22	21	22	22	22	-

Precipitation table from a climatic summary covering Poughkeepsie, New York.
(U.S. Weather Bureau)

height in feet above mean sea level. From these you will get a clear idea of the form of the land.

Knowing what weather to anticipate is just as important as knowing the terrain. For example, in the mountain regions of the southwestern United States, conditions for travel are usually favorable from June 15 through October 1. But in the mountains of the Pacific Northwest, the best times are from July 15 to September 15.

If you are unsure about the weather conditions of the area where you plan to travel, the U.S. Weather Bureau has records available that can help you. The Weather Bureau has prepared a series of booklets, one for each state or region, titled *Climatic Summary of the United States—Supplement for 1931 through 1952*. These are available from the Superintendent of Documents (U.S. Government Printing Office, Washington, D.C. 20402) for 20¢ to 70¢. Each booklet contains profiles of past weather of the region, giving highest, lowest and average temperatures, and detailed information as to precipitation.

As you begin to gather this information, you should also be preparing a list of every piece of clothing and equipment you plan to take. Keep reviewing the list to be sure that it contains only essential items. The chapters that follow are meant to guide you.

CHAPTER TWO
Equipment Basics

Backpacking requires several pieces of highly specialized equipment — the pack itself, a frame to secure it to your back, boots, a sleeping bag, and, if you expect to encounter very cold weather or snow, a tent.

The firms that manufacture these items and their principal retail outlets are listed in the appendix. If you don't live near a supplier, it doesn't matter because you can buy by mail. Don't overlook the major mail-order companies, Montgomery Ward and Sears.

Buy equipment of the very best quality, even if it means putting a severe strain on your budget. You can rationalize your expenditures in several ways. For one thing, the expenses are not for one trip or two or even a handful, but can be prorated over several years — and your initial outlay is virtually your only expense. Skiers have to buy lift tickets for as long as they ski and golfers have greens fees. But you'll never come upon a turnstile or ticket window in the woods.

If these reasons do not seem compelling enough, try to imagine yourself in the wilds when a piece of equipment breaks down or otherwise fails. Maybe a boot springs a leak or the stove fails to light. At that moment you would pay virtually any amount to solve the problem.

If you're undecided about a major purchase, renting may be a worthwhile alternative. Many retailers have packs, packframes and sleeping bags available on a trial-run basis. It will cost you about $20 to rent these three items for a weekend, and you'll need at least two or three times that amount as a deposit. Often rental fees can be applied toward the purchase of new gear.

Packframe and Packbag

For carrying moderate to heavy loads (those of thirty pounds or more) the only equipment to consider is the lightweight rigid packframe with its fitted packbag. This system distributes the load efficiently over your entire back, concentrating the weight on your hips and legs.

The packframe itself consists of a tubular aluminum structure whose flattened S shape fits to the contours of the shoulders, back and waist. I don't mean to imply that it rests upon your back. It doesn't. A pair of webbed nylon straps called backbands, each four to five inches in width and tautly stretched between the vertical members of the frame, hold the frame and its load away from the wearer's back.

A pair of padded straps, sometimes called a yoke or harness, pull the frame to the shoulders, while a padded waistband, known as a hipbelt or waistbelt, brings the load to the hips. It is this belt, which serves to place the weight of the load on the hips and legs, that has taken the drudgery out of backpacking. Both the harness and the waistbelt are adjustable.

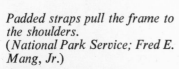

Padded straps pull the frame to the shoulders.
(*National Park Service; Fred E. Mang, Jr.*)

◀ *The lightweight packframe with its fitted packbag enables one to carry loads of thirty pounds and more over good distances with relative ease.*
(*U.S. Forest Service, Southwestern Region; Ray Manley*)

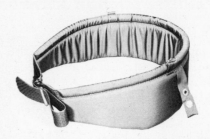

The padded hipbelt.
(*Camp Trails*)

Packframes come in different sizes. Kelty Pack, the firm that pioneered in the development of the body-contoured packframe, offers four sizes — ranging from small ("for persons of slight physique who expect to carry small, light loads") to extra large ("for persons of heavy physique who expect to carry large, heavy loads").

Your packbag should be big and durable and have at least two main compartments plus several small outer pockets.

The bigger the bag, the better, say the experts. The weight difference between the very largest and one of medium size is only about two ounces.

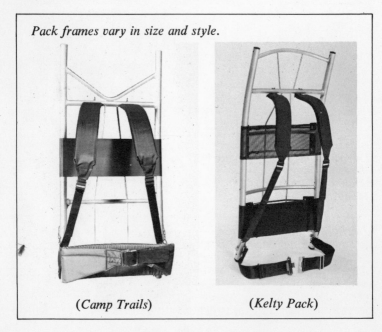

Pack frames vary in size and style.

(*Camp Trails*)   (*Kelty Pack*)

The type of fabric is important. It has to be tough enough to withstand constant chafing from brush and rocks, and it should also be waterproof (no fabric is really waterproof — water-repellent is what you will have to settle for). All zippers should be covered.

For convenience, the bag should have a minimum of six outer pockets with zippers and flaps. These are used for storing items you want to get to easily, such as an energy bar or maybe even the first-aid kit.

Naturally, the bag has to fit securely to the frame. This is usually accomplished by a series of grommets or clevis pins. A large packframe, including the harness and the waistband, plus the packbag, should weigh about four pounds.

The packframe system allows air to circulate between your back and the load. This ventilation is important insofar as your comfort is concerned. Another advantage of the packframe is its extreme versatility. Besides the packbag, you can lash just about anything you want to it — binoculars, your sleeping bag or a sectional fishing pole. For cold-weather camping, which entails a bulky (although not necessarily a heavy) load, the packframe system is a must.

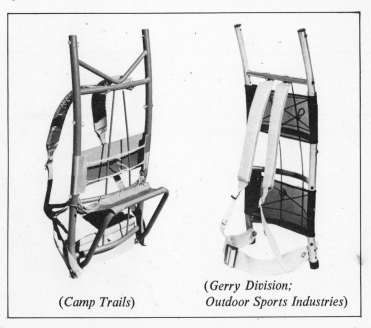

(Camp Trails)

(Gerry Division;
Outdoor Sports Industries)

Packbags, from small to large.

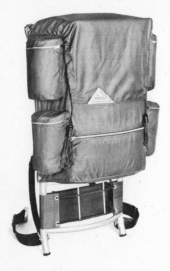

(*Kelty Packs*)

(*Gerry Division;
Outdoor Sports Industries*)

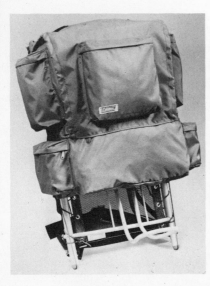

(*Coleman*)

The bigger the bag, the better

(Wenzel Company)

(Gerry Division;
Outdoor Sports Industries)

(Camp Trails)

(Camp Trails)

Frameless packs are suitable for shorter trips.

(Coleman)

(Gerry Division; Outdoor Sports Industries)

(Gerry Division; Outdoor Sports Industries)

(Gerry Division; Outdoor Sports Industries)

One accessory item you might possibly want to consider is the tumpline, or tump. It consists of an adjustable band that slings across the forehead and attaches to the sides of the packframe. The idea, of course, is to take some of the strain of the load off your back and shoulders. It's not something novices should get involved with, however.

Frameless Packs

On a one-day hike, there is no need to use the packframe and its related packbag. All you require is a small frameless bag which, like the packframe system, features padded shoulder straps and a waistband, but weighs only about one-and-a-half pounds. Such day packs are suitable for loads of up to twenty pounds.

The chief drawback of the frameless pack, aside from limited load it carries, is that it rides on the back. Thus it can generate a good deal of heat and can be uncomfortable on summer hikes.

Frame Packs

For loads between fifteen and thirty pounds, consider the pack with a built-in frame. It is often called a rucksack, although that term is sometimes applied to frameless packs, too. The frame pack is well suited for a couple on a weekend or even a week-long trip.

It employs many of the sample principles used in the packframe–backpack combination, including the shoulder harness and waistbelt. The frame prevents the load from resting on your back and provides ventilation. Some rucksacks have outer pockets.

One advantage that rucksacks have over the packframe system is that they do not catch in heavy brush. The legs of the packframe sometimes do.

Boots

Boots should be selected with the greatest care. Not only are they important in protecting your feet but they are necessary for the extra support required by the load you carry.

You can probably negotiate a good many miles wearing light-weight work boots or even sneakers, but there's really no sub-stitute for lug-soled trail boots. They protect your feet against bruises and abrasions you might sustain from roots or rocks, and insulate your feet from cold and dampness. They also give you secure footing over rocky terrain or loose stones.

There is such an enormous array of boots available that select-ing a suitable pair can be a difficult chore, yet there are certain

Buy top quality boots, made of leather, smooth and pliable, with lug soles and extra padding at the ankle.
(Bass Sports, Inc.)

guidelines that you can follow. Getting the proper height is easy. Seven inches is what most experts recommend. Anything beyond eight inches is going to constrict the muscles of your calf and cause problems.

As for material, leather is what you want. It should be smooth and pliable and of even texture. Beware of boots that have been dyed black or dark brown. Sometimes this is done to mask flaws or inferior leather. Highly polished boots, shiny like a dress shoe, aren't meant for outdoor wear.

The boots that you select should have as few seams as possible, and there should be padding beneath the tongue and at the ankle.

The uppers should be sturdy enough to give support to the muscles of your feet to help them bear the extra weight of your pack. They also should have some give to them, because your feet will spread slightly as you walk. The lugged rubber soles should be about one-half inch thick.

If you're going to be encountering extremely thick brush, you may be better off with knee boots. Very cold weather demands extra-thick boots. But these are extremes. For normal climate and average terrain, quality boots as described above are what you need.

Nylon laces are recommended over leather, and braided nylon is superior to the conventional flat or rounded laces. Leather laces absorb moisture, which causes innumerable difficulties.

Stay away from zippered boots. The zippers may work efficiently in the store, but outdoor use subjects them to possible damage. How do you repair a zipper in the woods?

Hooks can cause difficulty too. They get snagged in brush; they bend.

GETTING PROPER FIT   The matter of size is almost meaningless in getting fitted. The determining factor has to be how the boots feel.

In general, you must seek a snug fit — but be careful to allow enough room for the toes to move freely (a space of about one-half inch in front of the toes is sufficient). For a fit which is snug but not too tight, try this test. Unlace the boot, then stand erect and press your foot forward until the toes touch the end of the boot. There should be room enough for you to slide a finger into the gap between your heel and the boot.

Once the boot is laced, there should be virtually no movement in the heel area, neither side-to-side nor up-and-down; nor should you be able to slide your foot forward so that the toes touch at the front. Be sure you're standing erect when checking the heel fit.

It is more difficult to buy boots by mail order and expect to get a proper fit, yet tens of thousands do it every year. Firms that specialize in boots by mail order are listed in the appendix.

When buying by mail, don't order by size. Draw a silhouette of your foot and send it with your order. If the boots fail to fit properly, don't hesitate to return them.

New boots will be stiff and require breaking in. Wear them around the house and on short walks, working up to long hikes. Hitting the trail in new, stiff boots can lead to disaster.

Many authorities recommend soaking boots in water, then putting them on and walking around until the boots dry. The boots shape themselves to your foot. Don't try this with cheap boots, however.

INSOLES   Even with boots of high quality, the rough stitching within may chafe the bottom of your feet. You're not likely to notice these stitches at first but after five or six hours on the trail, they can become the source of real discomfort. The solution is an inner sole (or insole, for short). As the name suggests, it is an extra strip of material placed inside the boot. You can buy ready-made insoles at a shoe repair shop or at a drugstore.

Be wary of felt or foam insoles because they absorb perspiration and cause cold feet. Insoles of perforated plastic or nylon mesh are better; or you can cut your own out of shirt cardboard, but don't expect to get more than a day or two of wear out of these.

BOOT CARE   Wax your boots before you wear them, even before the break-in period. The wax waterproofs the leather and keeps it pliable. When cleaning is necessary, use saddle soap. Then coat the boots with a waterproofing compound.

If the boots should become wet, dry them slowly. Packing them with newspaper helps speed the drying process. Don't place them close to a fire or any other source of heat. Quick drying causes the soles to curl and, in general, is harmful to the leather.

When the soles wear out, have the boots resoled by an expert, perhaps by the firm from which you purchased them. Some companies sell soles separately, and advise taking the boots to a local shoe repair shop for resoling.

Boots should be of seamless leather, about seven inches in height. Wool socks of medium weight give maximum comfort. (National Park Service; Fred E. Mang, Jr.)

Quality boots can be made waterproof with a wax treatment. (National Park Service; Fred E. Mang, Jr.)

CAMP FOOTWEAR   At the end of the day, your feet deserve luxury treatment in the form of lightweight footwear. A pair of moccasins or sneakers should be on your equipment list. Be sure that the soles are reasonably thick.

Socks

If you query a dozen hikers, you are likely to get twelve different opinions on which type of boots are best, but with regard to socks they will all give you the same advice. Wool socks give maximum comfort, absorb sweat better and are more efficient from the standpoint of insulation. Nylon reinforcing at the toe and heel increases wearability, but don't permit any other compromises.

A new sock of proper size should be one-quarter to three-eighths of an inch longer than the foot when standing. After washing, there should be neither tightness nor looseness in the way it fits. Socks that are too large are likely to wrinkle and cause blisters. Those that are too tight reduce blood circulation and they also wear out quickly.

Really heavy socks aren't necessary. Socks of medium weight are what you want. Many hikers wear two pairs of socks, an inner lightweight pair of nylon or orlon, and an outer pair of wool that are heavier (and half a size larger). The idea of wearing two pairs is to reduce friction and keep the feet drier.

It may be difficult to wash socks daily because of a lack of water. In such cases, dry them thoroughly, then knead them between your hands to restore softness.

When you do wash them, use a mild soap or Woolite, never a detergent. Rinse thoroughly.

CHAPTER THREE
Clothing and Personal Gear

When you are hiking along the trail, your body is its own heater and air-conditioner. You can help it in both of these aspects by wearing the right kinds of clothing.

In warm weather your clothing should allow for a free flow of air through the fabric to carry off body heat. In winter your clothes should insulate, helping to retain body heat, but they also should permit evaporation of sweat. At all times, no matter what the season or temperature, your clothing should be comfortable and protect you from the sun and heavy brush.

For summer backpacking it's not likely you will need any special clothing (aside from hiking boots, discussed in the previous chapter). However, should you be anticipating any extremes in temperature or extended periods of wet weather, you will have to do some shopping.

If you feel you can pull together your backpacking wardrobe from what's available in your clothes closet, be sure that every item is in good condition. Don't take anything that's nearly

Underwear of fishnet construction is recommended.
(C. C. Valentine Co.)

worn out. Check each item of clothing and equipment carefully before you leave to be certain you're not going to have to make any repairs.

UNDERWEAR   Undershirts of fishnet construction are recommended for men. In hot weather, the net construction serves to hold your outside shirt away from your skin, allowing perspiration to evaporate. To cool off, you simply loosen the neck opening of your outer shirt, so as to permit the warm air to escape. Pulling out your shirttail will increase ventilation.

In cold weather, you do the opposite — close your shirt at the neck, tuck your shirttail in all around and button the sleeves. The air pockets within the individual net panels will then be heated by your body and help to keep you warm.

In really cold weather, wear long johns. Look for the two-layer type. A soft, itch-free cotton layer is next to the skin; the outer layer is wool or wool and nylon, and it acts as an insulator and also serves to dissipate perspiration. The air space between the two layers is also an insulator.

In warm weather, wear shorts. Your clothing should allow a free flow of air through the fabric.
(National Park Service; Fred E. Mang, Jr.)

For women, knit rayon or acetate underwear is recommended for warm-weather hiking; nylon is too hot. In cold weather, wear lightweight wool underwear.

SHIRTS   For warm weather, pick out a loosely-woven material that will absorb sweat, such as cotton or a cotton-wool mixture. Avoid the synthetics. Light colors are cooler than dark ones. A breast pocket with a button flap will have countless uses.

For cold weather, wear wool. It will keep you warm even if it gets wet.

PANTS   Blue jeans are fine, just as long as they don't fit too snugly. They are made of strong, tightly-woven material with a hard finish, and they're cuffless — the characteristics that hiking pants should have. One drawback jeans have is that they absorb water readily, take a long time to dry and they are apt to chafe when they are wet. For these reasons, the Appalachian Trail Conference recommends Grenfell cloth or Byrd cloth for pants. For cold weather walking, switch to wool in a whipcord weave.

Shorts are best for summer wear because they provide more efficient ventilation. But if you plan to wear shorts, bring long pants for cool evenings.

HAT   If your feet are cold, put on your hat. It's true. A snug fitting wool toque or wool cap, by preventing heat loss, will help to keep your entire body warm.

For summer wear you'll want a lightweight, broad-brimmed hat to protect you from the sun. The soft, flexible Crusher hat, which your local equipment shop may have, weighs about three ounces. Poplin hats are fine, too.

GLOVES   Don't forget light woolen gloves or fleece-lined leather gloves if you expect cold winds or near-freezing temperatures.

Rainwear

It's always wise to pack along protection against the rain. If you know the area and anticipate only infrequent showers, a lightweight plastic sheet will probably suffice. When the rain comes, sit down someplace, pull the plastic about your head and sit it out.

A poncho is much better protection but it weighs more, about ten ounces for a nylon one, and up to two and one-half pounds for the rubberized type. The advantage of the poncho is that its hood fits snugly about your head and it has snap fasteners that prevent it from being blown about. Thus, you're able to keep moving. Some ponchos are extra long so as to fit over the pack.

At Admiralty Island, Alaska, hikers cover packs with plastic covers.
(*U. S. Forest Service; Alaska Region*)

Down-filled Clothing

Down-filled clothing offers the greatest warmth at the least weight and can be packed into a very small space. The various down-filled garments now available cover a wide range in style and price, but no matter what the item there is one feature that you should always check — the seams. Does the garment have sewn-through seams or baffled seams (see diagram, p. 87)?

With the former, there is no thickness. Wherever there is a seam, therefore, there is no insulation. Look for baffled seams.

Your parka should be both windproof and waterproof.
(Sierra Designs)

DOWN-FILLED PARKA   Your parka — essentially a hooded jacket — should be both waterproof and windproof. No parka is wholly waterproof but select one that is at least highly water repellent.

Windproofing is just as important. In this regard, the wind-chill factor (see the chart below) is something to consider. If the wind velocity is thirty miles per hour when the temperature is 30°F, it's the same as if the temperature was −1°F.

						Temperature (°F)				
		70	60	50	40	30	20	10	0	−10
Wind Velocity	0	70	60	50	40	30	20	10	0	−10
(MPH)	5	69	58	48	37	27	16	6	−5	−15
	10	63	51	40	28	16	4	−9	−21	−33
	15	61	48	36	21	10	−4	−18	−32	−45
	20	59	45	32	19	5	−10	−25	−39	−53
	25	58	44	30	16	3	−14	−30	−44	−59
	30	57	43	28	14	−1	−17	−34	−48	−63
	35	56	42	27	12	−3	−19	−36	−51	−66
	40	55	41	26	11	−4	−21	−38	−53	−69

A windproof parka solves the wind-chill problem, for it reduces the wind velocity at the skin to zero or very close to it. Strenuous activity will generate more heat, which will be retained if the parka insulates properly.

To be windproof, the parka's hood should be an integral part of the garment. You should be able to close the hood to your face by means of a drawstring. There should be a drawstring at the waist, too, and the sleeves should close at the wrist.

It's usually wise to buy a parka that is a size larger than your normal jacket size because you'll be wearing several layers of clothing underneath. Down-filled parkas range in price from $60 to $80.

DOWN-FILLED JACKETS   Down-filled parkas are for extremely cold weather and bitter wind; down jackets are for merely cold weather. A quality down-filled jacket gives greater warmth than the heaviest wool yet weighs less than the lighest cashmere sweater. Most are available with detachable hoods. Jackets range in price from $25 to almost $50.

Sweater jackets and super sweaters look like jackets but are lighter in weight and less expensive than the real thing.

Down-filled jackets.
(*Sierra Designs*)

VESTS Sleeveless and always constructed with sewn-through seams, vests are designed to be worn under other garments. Because they are extremely light in weight — some models weigh only twelve or thirteen ounces — and take up such a small amount of space when packed, they are much more practical than a wool sweater. Vests cost a bit less than $20.

DOWN-FILLED BOOTIES For people whose feet get cold, these are meant to be worn in the sleeping bag, in the tent or around the campsite. They cost about $8.50.

A down sweater.
(Sierra Designs)

Down vests are sleeveless
and of sewn-through con-
struction.
(Woolrich Woolen Mills)

Personal Gear

Such topics as washing yourself and whether you're going to shave are very much your own affair. The personal items listed on the pages that follow are merely suggestions.

SOAP A four-ounce bar of toilet soap should last the better part of two weeks, so if you're planning a trip of shorter duration take only half a bar. Depending on what part of the country you're trekking, you may have to be concerned about getting a soap that will lather. Vel is one brand that I recommend.

TOWEL, WASHCLOTH You'll want to take a small hand towel for drying off after swimming, and a washcloth for the usual reasons.

TOOTHBRUSH Take your toothbrush from home and pack it in a small plastic bag or wrap the bristle end in a square of aluminum foil. You may have read of backpackers who saw off part of the toothbrush handle to cut down on weight. Don't bother. The entire handle doesn't weigh as much as half an ounce.

Don't carry toothpaste; use salt. You can also clean your teeth effectively with bar soap. You may be surprised to find how clean and refreshed it leaves your mouth. But first try it at home.

TOILET TISSUE You may be thinking in terms of toilet tissue that comes in squares as being more convenient to pack. However, a roll is much easier to handle. A full roll weighs about eight ounces. Be sure to pack it in a plastic bag.

COMB; NAIL FILE (OR CLIPPER); NAIL BRUSH

SHAVING GEAR This, of course, is optional. Often those who take along shaving cream, a razor and the rest, don't bother to shave.

INSECT REPELLENT Whether you'll require something to ward off insects depends on where you'll be traveling and at what time of the year. In lake country in the late summer, mosquitoes may attack you with terrible ferocity. Use a stick repellent of cream from a tube in preference to a liquid.

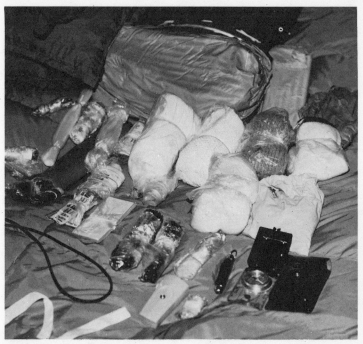

Pack personal gear in individual plastic bags.
(*National Park Service Photo; Fred E. Mang, Jr.*)

SUN PROTECTION   Even if you wear a broad-brimmed hat, your face and lips will need protection from the sun and wind. This is especially true if you're going to be climbing high mountain peaks, so high that the air begins to thin. Many equipment dealers now stock Glacier Cream to protect the face and hands, but new products are coming on the market all the time. Consult your neighborhood pharmacist.

SEWING KIT   A few needles and several two- or three-foot lengths of nylon thread are essential for emergency repairs, like stitching up a tear in tent fabric or replacing a button. Pre-thread the needles. Needles are also valuable as a first-air item (see below), so take along a good supply.

SAFETY PINS   Take several, medium sized. They are often valuable in making emergency repairs and can be also used in clothespin fashion to hang socks and other items out to dry.

Miscellaneous Equipment Items

Under miscellaneous, list whatever recreational gear you plan to take — a camera and film, fishing equipment, reading material or perhaps writing gear.

Also plan to bring the following:

ROPE   You'll find countless uses for forty to fifty feet of stout, braided, nylon cord (parachute cord) one-eighth inch in diameter. A piece of it serves as clothesline or you can use a longer length as the ridge rope for your tent. Use short pieces to hang cooking pots over the fire or as emergency lacing for a boot.

FLASHLIGHT   You will probably require about five minutes of intermittent artificial light every twenty-four hours, which means that your flashlight doesn't have to be a large, heavy-duty one. If you follow a conventional schedule, you will have eaten your evening meal, performed the cleanup chores and prepared your bed site before dark. You'll need some light to find your way from the campfire to your sleeping bag, and perhaps a beam or two to untie a knotted shoelace or to aid you in stowing away your outer clothing. It will be daylight when you awaken.

A standard two-cell flashlight using "D" batteries is all you require. It weighs about ten ounces. If you're trying to cut back on weight, you may make do with a "C" size flashlight, which weighs about five ounces, or even a penlight, which uses "AA" batteries.

For each three or four days of your trip, carry an extra pair of batteries. Be sure to also carry spare bulbs.

Before you set out in the morning, open the flashlight and reverse the lower battery. This will prevent battery power from draining away if you accidentally switch the flashlight on during the day.

MIRROR   Bring a small mirror to use as a signalling device in case you get lost (on a sunny day).

SUNGLASSES   Eyeglasses with tinted or polarized lenses will make your walking more enjoyable anytime, and they're a must should the ground be snow-covered.

You may also want to bring an axe, a pedometer, a jackknife or handkerchiefs (you can use toilet paper), but veteran backpackers consider these to be marginal items.

First-Aid Kit

You can purchase a ready-made first-aid kit at your corner pharmacy, but it's more practical to make up your own, with the contents suited to your personal needs and the terrain you'll be traveling. Here are some suggestions as to what it might contain.

four three-inch-square gauze pads
one roll of one-inch adhesive tape
one dozen Band-Aids
ammonia inhalant, one or two small vials
one dozen Aspirin tablets — for headaches
several needles — for breaking blisters, removing slivers
twelve moleskin patches
first-aid instruction manual

You don't need a heavy plastic case for these items. A double-weight plastic bag will do nicely.

You may also want to take along an antiseptic, such as tincture of iodine or Merthiolate. Bear in mind, however, while it's true these are commonly used for treating minor cuts and lacerations, besides killing germs they also frequently kill tissue. Germs, some of which are always present, multiply quickly in devitalized tissue. So antiseptic solutions sometimes actually delay healing. This is eminently true in the case of the backpacker trekking the remote wilds, whose hygienic routine has been drastically altered.

The best way to treat a scratch or laceration is to wash it thoroughly with soap and water; dry it, and then apply a dressing.

Moleskin patches are discussed in Chapter Four. Applied to the foot or a toe at the first sign of soreness, a patch will help keep a blister from forming. If you know from past experience where trouble spots are likely to develop, you can apply patches before you set out.

"First-aid instruction manual" on the above list refers to any handbook concerning emergency treatment that you might conceivably have to administer during your trip. The American Red Cross *First Aid Textbook* is often recommended; however, it has

become outdated in many aspects. A modern and more practical
guide is one titled, *Being Your Own Wilderness Doctor*, by Russel
Kodet and Bradford Angier (Stackpole Books, 1968; $3.95).

Another source of helpful advice, not nearly as comprehensive
but certainly adequate, is an information sheet available through
the American National Red Cross titled, "First Aid at a Glance,"
It's free; call your local Red Cross Office and request one.

Some optional items you might consider include a mild laxa-

Poison ivy grows in three-leaf clusters.

tive, either milk of magnesia tablets or a few squares of choco-lated Ex-Lax. These are sometimes needed in the first day or two of the trip when your body is beginning to adjust to new foods and different water.

Mineral oil can also be used as a laxative and it has many other uses. In a pinch it can be used as a fire starter or a cooking oil, and you can use it to waterproof your boots. Vaseline — buy the tube — is another item with a variety of uses, one important one being in the treatment of minor burns.

If you are carrying any meat that might be subject to spoilage, remember that tainted food can cause diarrhea. The treatment for this is paregoric, or Lomotil, which is available in tablet form.

If your trip is going to be much more than a week or so in length, it's wise to take along a dozen tetracycline capsules to combat any serious infection. A wide-spectrum antibiotic, tetra-cycline costs about 20¢ a capsule. Ask your neighborhood pharmacist how long their potency will remain. You may have to replace them every year or so.

An ointment to relieve muscle soreness, such as Ben-Gay or Heet, is another optional item. As a general rule, don't use such preparations in cold weather if they make you sweat, which could worsen the condition. Intracel, a liquid, might be con-sidered instead. Check with your pharmacist.

If you know yourself to be allergic to insect bites or bee stings be sure to include whatever counteractant your physician has prescribed. Benadryl is one drug often used in this regard.

Rubbing alcohol is an effective treatment for skin rashes de-rived from poisonous plants. Wash the infected area thoroughly with soap and water, then rinse with alcohol. Remove and wash any clothing worn during contact. Carry the rubbing alcohol, mineral oil or any liquid in a small polyethelene bottle or one of the new aluminum bottles. These are so light in weight they seem helium filled and they're just as durable as plastic containers.

The new cortisone sprays have proven extremely effective in relieving itching and swelling caused by poison ivy. Of course, the wisest thing to do is to learn to recognize poisonous plants and avoid them. Poison ivy has leaves that are smooth, glossy and waxy in appearance. They grow in clusters of three. In the fall, the plant bears white berries. Poison oak is similar but the leaves have the familiar oak shape.

Poison sumac, which is common to the southeastern United States, grows to shrub height. It has small leaves growing from a single stalk and small greenish-white berries.

CHAPTER FOUR
On the Trail

How much weight should you carry? During World War II, the average American foot soldier was believed to be capable of toting fifty to seventy-five pounds, and Himalayan Sherpas are known for their ability to carry a load equal to their own weight for the entire day. The military services now realize that the infantrymen of the 1940's were overburdened, and Sir John Hunt, who lead the first successful Mount Everest climb, found Sherpa bearers covered greater distances at faster speeds, were more efficient overall, when their loads were limited to forty-five pounds.

In other words, don't toil. You can be wearing the best boots money can buy, have had your packframe fitted by Colin Fletcher ("the country's leading authority on walking," according to publisher Alfred A. Knopf), and be blessed with perfect weather, but an overloaded pack will dampen your joy as quickly as a foot blister.

Know precisely how much weight constitutes a real burden for you. As a rule of thumb, set a limit of between one-fourth to one-third of your body weight. In the booklet, *Backpacking in the National Forest Wilderness*, which describes a typical family's trail experiences, the father started with a fifty-one-pound pack, and the mother with one of thirty-eight pounds. The seventeen-year-old son also carried thirty-eight pounds, while the eleven-year-old daughter took twenty-six pounds.

Experiment. By trial and error you'll find the maximum weight you can tote comfortably.

One other word about weight — the load gets lighter as the hike progresses. Each day you use up food and other items.

Loading Up

As you organize your load and stow it in your pack, your basic objective should be to place the bulk of the load as high and as far forward toward the shoulders as is possible. You will, however, want to make some compromises for the sake of comfort and convenience.

A person's center of gravity runs along the spine and through the legs to the ground. When you walk, you balance your weight along this line of force. To carry additional weight and do it efficiently, you must bring it as close to the line as you possible can; otherwise the weight of the load will pull you off balance. The ankles are a pivot point for balance. The further an object is from the pivot point, the easier it is to balance. It is for these reasons that you should seek to keep the load as far forward and as high as you can.

To load the bag, lay it flat on the ground, the mouth toward you. Place the heaviest objects in the bag first, concentrating them toward the mouth. Medium-weight objects should go in next, and the lightest objects last.

But it is not likely you will want to follow this advice to the letter. For instance, if you anticipate rain, you won't be stowing the poncho in the bottom of the bag. You'll quickly learn, also, that an item like a stove is not to be placed in the bag first, despite its weight. A stove's sharp corners can poke through the bag into your shoulder.

As this may suggest, the skill of packing is largely acquired through trial and error. How you stow your gear varies from trip to trip, and from day to day, depending on your requirements.

Pack the outer pockets with items which are going to be in frequent use — your compass, knife, matches (in a waterproof

Pack compartments and pockets should be packed so that heavier items are toward the top and seldom used items at the bottom of the bag. Pockets should be used for items that are frequently needed. One firm — Himalayan Back Packs — gives the following suggestions.

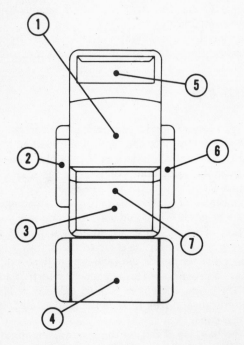

1 — UPPER COMPARTMENT. *Cooking gear, food packets and tent (depending on type).*

2 — SIDE POCKET. *Toilet kit (toothbrush, soap, toilet paper), flashlight or candle, poncho.*

3 — LOWER COMPARTMENT. *Air mattress or sleeping pad, ground cloth, tent (if lightweight), windbreaker jacket, extra socks and extra clothing.*

4 — STUFF BAG. *Sleeping bag.*

5 — FLAP POCKET *Maps, fire permit, fishing license, notebook, pencil, identification.*

6 — SIDE POCKET. *First aid supplies, sunburn creams, insect repellent, water purification tablets, matchsafe, canteen.*

7 — BACK POCKET. *Eating utensils, drinking cup, waterproof matches, sunglasses, and lunch and trail snacks.*

case), map (in a plastic bag), toilet paper (also in a plastic bag), meat bars and other nibbles, suntan lotion and foot powder. Your own list will contain many other items in addition to these.

It's not critical which item goes in what pocket. But what is important is that you develop a system and stick with it. Otherwise, there's no advantage in having multiple pockets.

You may find it comfortable to vary the position of the packbag in keeping with the terrain you are covering. Having the packbag high on the frame with the cylinder-shaped stuff bag (see Chapter Seven) beneath it, is considered the best arrangement for most conditions. When you encounter rugged terrain or you begin to climb, lower the position of the packbag, securing the stuff bag above it. This will give you greater stability and make walking easier.

Hoisting the Pack

The easiest way to get into the pack is to have someone hold it for you as you slip your arms through the shoulder straps. If you're by yourself, position the pack on a fallen tree, a stump or a rock ledge.

Often, however, there will be no raised surface that you can use. In such cases, swing the pack onto a raised thigh, and then slip one shoulder through its related shoulder strap. Holding one leg of the packframe, raise the load a bit higher, and then slip the other arm through.

This is difficult to do if the load is a heavy one, say, fifty pounds or so. Then you will have to sit down, get into the shoulder straps, adjust the waistbelt, and then roll to one side and clamber to your feet. It is every bit as awkward as it sounds but there is no known alternative.

How to Hike

During your first day or two on the trail, take it easy; don't push yourself. This should be a period of orientation, a time spent in getting used to your load and establishing a routine.

As you walk along, seek to develop a swinging gait — a rhythmic manner of moving that will allow you to cover mile after mile with ease and comfort.

Unfortunately, the art of walking has gone the way of good

penmanship and the curtsy. You should point your toes straight ahead on every step. Come down lightly on the heel, reach forward with your toes and use them to push off.

Equally important, set a pace that you can maintain throughout the day. Your rest stops should be evenly spaced, perhaps one ten-minute stop every hour. Your goal should be to arrive at your destination with the strength and energy to prepare and enjoy a comfortable camp. The important word is *enjoy*.

When you stop to rest during the day, relax as completely as you can. Take off your pack. Prop it against a rock or a tree and lean back against it. You may even want to doze for a few minutes.

Many guidebooks will tell you that your average pace will be approximately two miles an hour, but don't put much credence in this statistic. For one thing, no two people walk at exactly the same speed. The size of the load you're carrying and the terrain are other important considerations. Along a flat, straight roadway, you probably will be able to maintain, even exceed, the two-mile-an-hour pace. But the miles of flat, straight roadway which you will encounter are likely to be very few in number.

When you stop to rest, stretch out; relax; doze.
(National Park Service Photo; Fred E. Mang, Jr.)

On level terrain, you may be able to maintain a two-mile-an-hour pace.
(National Park Service Photo; Fred E. Mang, Jr.)

In rough country you will be lucky to maintain a pace of half-a-mile an hour, and if you are climbing you will have all you can do to negotiate a thousand feet in an hour without running out of breath.

What you should be concerned about is how you walk, the rhythm, the pace, not how far. Once you have developed a pace that you can maintain throughout the day, the miles will take care of themselves.

Foot Care

Even if your boots are of the highest quality and perfectly
fitted, you may encounter some foot problems on the trail. Conditioning your feet before setting out on a long trek with a heavy
load is the best way to avoid trouble.

During the time you are breaking in your boots, you will also
be toughening up your feet. Walk enough during the conditioning period so that the skin hardens in any area which rubs
against the boot.

A daily application of rubbing alcohol during the week preced-
ing the hike is helpful. The alcohol kills bacteria, thus making the
skin more healthy, and it speeds the evaporation of perspiration,
hastening the skin-hardening process. Foot powder, which helps
to keep the feet dry, is helpful, but not as effective as alcohol.
Don't use conventional talcum powder, which contains ingredients that serve to soften the skin.

Once you set out, keep your feet dry. People who perspire a
good deal should not allow their socks to become sweat-soaked.
Change to a dry pair.

Don't hesitate to give your feet a breather during the day. Stop,
remove your boots and rub your feet vigorously. If there's water
nearby, soak them for a minute or two. Dry them thoroughly and
put on clean socks, which can be sprinkled with foot powder,
before setting out again. Repeat the treatment anytime you begin
to get foot weary.

A blister is a major catastrophe, an affliction that can all but
cripple you for as long as a week. At the first suggestion of soreness, stop immediately and get your boot off for an examination.
Any reddened area indicates where a blister is going to form.
Cover the spot with a Band-Aid; a piece of moleskin plaster is
even better. Inquire about the latter at your local pharmacy.

A blister may be caused by a tiny stone that works its way into
the shoe, a wrinkle in one's sock or, as is usually the case, by an
ill-fitting boot. If the boot toe is not large enough or too stiff, the
tops of the toes, or the top of a toe, is likely to blister. If the boot
is too short or laced too loosely, the end of the toes may blister.

A boot that is too narrow causes blistering on the outside of
either the little or big toes. The heel is subject to blisters when the
boot is laced too loosely or the heel space is too large.

If a blister does form, wash the area with soap and water and
then follow this treatment, prescribed by the U.S. Army for its

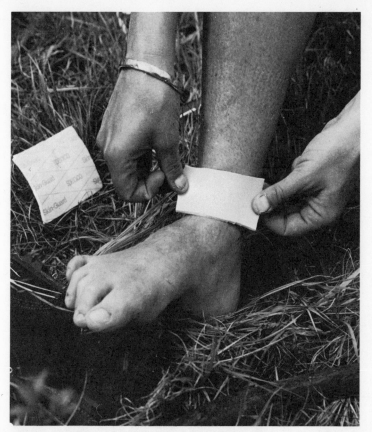

A blister requires careful, thoughtful treatment.
(*National Park Service Photo; Fred E. Mang, Jr.*)

foot soldiers. "Empty the blister, if unbroken, by pricking the lower edge with a needle or knifepoint which has been held in a flame. Do not remove the skin, but cover the blister with an absorbent adhesive bandage or similar dressing smoothly applied with adhesive plaster extending beyond its edge. After applying the dressing, dust the outside and entire foot with foot powder." For the absorbent adhesive bandage, I suggest moleskin.

Blisters are evidence you did not prepare properly. You may have not been careful enough in selecting your boots or perhaps your conditioning program was inadequate. Or it may be that you failed to heed the first signs of foot soreness. Hardly ever are blisters the result of plain misfortune.

Trail Safety

"People not experienced in wilderness survival have no idea how to cope when they get in trouble," says a National Park ranger. "Their first-aid tools in city life — a phone call, a credit card, or a check — won't buy them much in the woods. Out here, the rules of the game change."

Indeed, it is true. No one knows for sure how many people die in the wilderness, but in the national parks and forests, fatalities total about one hundred a year. These result from falls, burns,

Filling out a registration slip at an entrance to the Gates of the Mountains Wilderness Area in the Helena National Forest. (*U.S.D.A. Forest Service; Philip G. Schlamp*)

exposure, avalanches and drowning. Thousands more are injured.

In February 1972, nineteen-year-old Jeffrey Hayes and two teenage friends climbed into a Jeep and started up Braddock Mountain, near Frederick, Maryland, when the worst storm of the winter came howling out of the northeast. When the Jeep became bogged down in heavy snow, his companions retreated to try another route, but Jeffrey set out on foot, saying he'd meet his friends at the top. He was never seen alive again.

When Jeffrey's friends finally reached the top, they could not find him. They walked down the road he was to have traveled and found his footprints but they eventually faded in the drifting snow.

As the blizzard raged on, phone calls by the hundreds poured into park rangers, the state police, and the local game warden as people sought information on missing relatives or emergency transportation to hospitals. Countless stranded motorists called for help. The emergency call placed by Jeffrey Hayes' two companions was just one more problem for overworked officials.

About three hours after the call was received, local police dispatched a helicopter to Braddock Mountain. But it was too dark to see anything. Police called off the search until morning when rescue parties began combing the area. Around noontime they found Jeffrey's body. He had frozen to death.

A state trooper assigned to investigate the young man's death had the following comments: "People not properly trained and dressed, who go off in bad weather, are bound to get in trouble. With low visibility, you get disoriented. The experienced hiker knows how to pick out landmarks and walk a straight line. The inexperienced tends to travel in circles. From the footprints, Hayes did not make it to the top. But for some reason he started back down again and that's when he got lost."

As this tragedy points up, entering a wilderness area can be just as hazardous as jaywalking in heavy traffic. You must observe certain safety rules.

Before you set out, be certain to inform a reliable person as to when you plan to return, the day and the hour. If you plan to hike in National Park or Forest or a state forest, give this information to a ranger. A map that details the route that you plan to follow could be of additional help. If you should lose your way and people start looking for you, you want them to have something specific to go on. Once you set a return date and time, stick to it — for obvious reasons.

Learn to be observant on the trail. Remember your route. Keep track of landmarks, of streams and mountains and the lay of the land. Keep track of the time.

If you should lose your way and become separated from your companions, sit down and rest. Wait. Build a signal fire. Your friends will be looking for you in a few hours. Above all, *stay put* — even it•it means waiting a day or two.

If you don't expect anyone to come looking for you because your whereabouts are not known, push on slowly, deliberately. Take plenty of time to reconstruct your route using your map and compass (see below). Try to find a high point that will give you a general view of the area.

If you remain lost, follow drainage downstream. In most areas this will bring you to a trail, road or power transmission line. In canyon country it's usually wise to follow a ridge uphill until you reach a natural shelter among trees or rocks. Then build a signal fire.

The National Park Service rules of the road for those entering a wilderness area are as follows:

(1) Always carry matches. Know how to start a fire, and how to put it out.

(2) Learn which clothes are merely bulk, and which ones will keep you warm. A hat, for instance, will go a long way toward keeping the whole body warm.

(3) Know what types of muscular activity can increase the metabolic rate the most. Muscular tension exercises and shivering are more expedient than stomping around. Nicotine can cause cold fingers.

(4) Know what foods increase body heat production.

(5) Recognize that the need for water is about two quarts a day, but is doubled by excessive perspiration or by the drying effects of high altitudes.

(6) If tent shelters are not available, know how to use snow, ice and tree branches for protection against wind and storms.

(7) Study up on avalanches. Accident reports show that most victims started the snow tumbling themselves.

(8) Never go exploring without maps and a compass.

(9) Don't travel alone or separate from a group.

(10) On trails, be familiar with the habits of the area's animals.

Many equipment stores sell survival kits like these.
(Survival Systems, Inc.)

The Compass and How to Use It

Tests conducted by the U.S. Army have shown that it is almost impossible for a person to walk a straight line without some type of navigational instrument. Men with varying amounts of outdoor experience were blindfolded and instructed to walk a straight line in an open plain. The blindfolds prevented them from seeing the sun and there was no wind to give them a clue as to direction. In the course of the experiment, some men walked to the right, some to the left; not one walked in a straight line.

It's for this reason that you should equip yourself with a compass and know how to use it. Buy one that's rugged, that can take some abuse. A sturdy case will help in this regard. More expensive compasses contain a glycerin-type liquid in which the needle seems to float as it turns. Consider this unnecessary.

You might, however, want to consider buying a sighting compass, a type which can be aimed at a particular object. In following map courses, this type is simpler to use than the more conventional compasses.

A good compass, used in combination with a Geographical Survey map, can be an invaluable navigational aid.
(*National Park Service Photo; Fred E. Mang, Jr.*)

A compass is not a precision instrument. It consists essentially of a pointer needle, magnetized at one end, and mounted on a central post over a dial marked with various directions. When the compass is laid flat, the needle lines up with the north magnetic pole, which is located in north central Canada about 1,300 miles south of the geographical north pole. Only rarely does the direction in which the compass points coincide with a true north and south meridian. In fact, only when you are on a line directly north or south of Cincinnati, Ohio, will the compass indicate true north. In some parts of northeastern Canada, the compass needle points directly to the west, and in northwestern Canada it points east.

The angle between the geographic north-south line and the local magnetic meridian is called magnetic declination, and is expressed in degrees, plus (+) to the east and minus (−) to the west. U.S.G.S. topographic maps express compass variations in

Hikers stop to consult a map before entering California's Angeles National Forest. (U.S. Forest Service)

this manner. Some compasses are fitted with declination offset devices.

If your compass is not so equipped, be sure to make the compensation yourself. Most people are aware that magnetic declination exists but they believe that the amount of error is negligible. It's not; every degree of difference between the direction in which the compass needle points and true north will lead you off your route by one foot in every sixty feet. A variation of fifteen degrees (which is about the magnetic declination for New York City) would throw you off by one-third of a mile for every two miles you travel.

When you take a compass reading, you also have to be aware that the needle's movement can be affected by nearby iron and steel objects. A knife, an axe, a wire fence or a steel rail, even your belt buckle, can cause errors. Some compasses are shielded against such interference.

There may come a time when you wish to travel across a section of land where there are no trails or guideposts. Snow or dense fog may cut visibility to next to nothing. In such cases a compass is invaluable. First, draw a line on your map connecting the point where you are located and your destination. Using your compass find the direction of the line and then follow that route.

Once you know the direction in which you're heading, you can use the compass to steer you back. Suppose your outward-bound course was 42°. For the reverse course, obtain a reading on the compass dial and then add 180°. This would give you a course of 222°.

When your first heading is more than 180°, you have to subtract 180° to get the reverse heading. If your initial heading was 240°, your return course would be 60° — 240° minus 180°.

One way to keep on course without a compass is to locate two landmarks on a line in the direction you want to walk. As you move toward the first, keep it lined up with the second. As you are about to reach the first landmark, pick out a third, one that lies on a line with the other two. Keep this up, always picking out a third landmark just before reaching the first, and you will hue to a straight line.

Maps take a beating on the trail. One method of preservation is to cut the map apart on the lines of longitude and latitude and reassemble the pieces on a square of muslin, leaving a narrow space between each section. Paste them in place with rubber cement. This will permit you to fold and unfold the map countless times without damaging it. Another way to protect your map is to carry it in an acetate envelope, which you can buy in a stationery store.

Snakes

"Remain calm" is the first piece of advice that first-aid manuals have for snakebite victims. Of course, it's almost impossible to follow. At any rate, have the patient lie down and stay as quiet as possible. This is to decelerate blood circulation and the spread of venom.

The traditional method of emergency treatment is to tie a constricting bandage a few inches above the wound, and then with a razor blade or razor-sharp knife make a small X-shaped cut through the fang puncture or punctures. Some instruction manuals recommend an H-shaped cut. But the idea is to induce bleeding which will flush the venom away.

To accomplish this treatment, sporting goods stores sell snakebite kits. The most widely known is the Cutter Compak Suction Kit, which is made up of a sharp blade, sterilizing liquid, a tourniquet and three suction cups for drawing out the venom. The kit, which costs about $3, is indeed compact, taking up about as much space as a four-inch candle. Complete instructions are packed with the kit.

Of course, the best treatment of all is to get the victim to a doctor as quickly as possible so that an antivenin can be administered. What you must never do is give the victim alcohol. It stimulates the heartbeat and thus spreads the venom.

Most poisonous snakes in the United States are to be found in the West. They include copperheads, cottonmouths (water moccasins) and rattlesnakes. Coral snakes, common to the

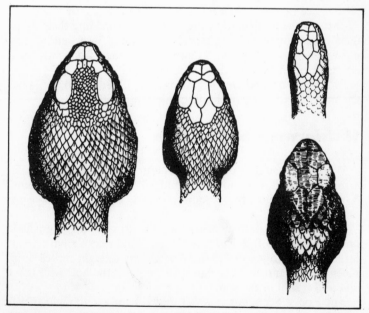

Poisonous snakes can be recognized by their arrow-shaped heads (formed by the poison sacs in their jowls). Snakes shown here are (left to right) rattlesnake, copperhead and water moccasin. Coral snake is at upper right.

southern United States, are poisonous, but they rarely bite humans.

Learn to recognize these snakes. The distinguishing feature of copperheads, cottonmouths and rattlesnakes is an arrow-shaped head.

The copperhead has the coppery color for which it is named and irregularly shaped reddish-brown markings. The cottonmouth is somewhat similar in appearance, although larger. When aroused, it lifts its head and opens its mouth wide to reveal a cotton-white area within.

The coral snake is slender, with a small head and brilliant markings — a black band, yellow band and coral-red band. The harmless harlequin or bead snake is similar in size to the coral snake, but has red and black bands only.

There are about thirty different species of rattlesnakes but all bear a pattern of dark bands on a lighter background. Eastern diamondbacks are the biggest rattlers, measuring up to eight feet in length and weighing as much as thirty pounds. But most rattlers are no more than three or four feet in length.

Rattlers are particularly dangerous when shedding their skins; they are blind during this period and will lash out at any movement close to them. Young rattlers shed frequently, and adults as often as three times a year.

Snakes in Fact and Fiction (Macmillan, 1958; $4.95), by James Oliver, is an informative book on this topic.

Wilderness Sanitation

When you rough it in the backcountry, you are without television, without refrigeration — and without indoor plumbing. You can't, however, forget sanitation. The rules of good hygiene demand it.

Wilderness sanitation means cat sanitation — digging a hole and covering up feces afterward. The hole doesn't have to be large — eight to ten inches in diameter, six to eight inches deep. Keep the sod intact if you can. After use, fill the hole with loose soil and tramp in the sod.

The Forest Service points out that the top six to eight inches of soil acts as a biological disposer which decomposes organic material in a few days.

Consideration

"Take nothing but pictures. Leave nothing but footprints." This is the advice that The Wilderness Society has for those who enter the backcountry.

It's unpardonable to vandalize a trail, befoul a stream or lake, or leave litter at a campsite.

The once almost limitless wilderness that made up the American frontier has shrunk to be about 2 percent of its former size. Unless those who enter the backcountry use it with discretion, these last vestiges will disappear, too.

CHAPTER FIVE
Trail Foods

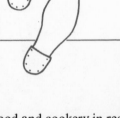

There's been a revolution in trail food and cookery in recent years with the result that on an extended trip it is now possible to enjoy a wide variety of highly nutritional meals that are easy to prepare and eminently palatable, if not downright tasty.

Freeze-drying is what is behind the revolution. Foods are now dehydrated at very low temperatures, as low as −50°F, a process that serves to lock in all the natural food goodness and flavor. Such foods have the added advantage of being extremely light in weight and have little bulk. You can carry a foil envelope containing the equivalent of a ten-pound sack of potatoes in one corner of your pack and hardly know it's there.

The technical term for the processes that accomplishes these things is vacuum sublimation. According to Oregon Freeze Dry Foods, one of the largest suppliers of meals for backpackers, this is how it works. Imagine that you had a block of ice that you wanted to change to water vapor. Normally you would apply heat and first melt the ice changing it into liquid water, then continue to heat the water until it started to boil. Eventually, it would all boil away as steam.

Vacuum sublimation is entirely different. The block of ice is placed in a large chamber and the pressure is reduced to a nearly perfect vacuum. Then radiant heat is applied to the block of ice. Now a strange thing happens. The ice does not turn into water which has to be boiled away. Instead the solid ice turns into water vapor.

This is how foods are freeze-dried. First, fresh cooked food is flash frozen. Next, it is placed into vacuum chambers where the ice is vacuumed away. Then the food is packaged.

This process lends itself not only to individual fruits and vegetables, but to much more elaborate dishes. In the deepest backcountry you can treat yourself to a dinner of beef stroganoff or chicken tetrazzini, lunches of hamburgers or tuna salad, and breakfasts featuring eggs in any one of half a dozen different forms. In each case, the directions on the packet state, "Add water and heat." What could be simpler?

The firms that specialize in freeze-dried foods for back-packers are listed in the appendix. You can obtain detailed in-

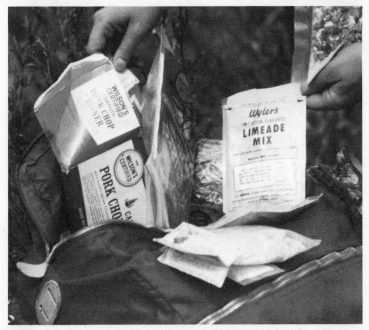

Freeze-dried foods have revolutionized camp food and cookery.
(National Park Service Photo; Fred E. Mang, Jr.)

"Just add water and heat," say the packet directions.
(*Dri Lite Foods*)

formation concerning the meal packets each has available. Of
course, much of your food purchasing can be done at your local
supermarket, for such items as powdered drinks, dried fruits,
cereal, coffee, tea, etc.

Getting Nutritional Value

The first thing to consider in meal planning is not package
weight, ease of preparation or palatability; it's nutritional value.
You should consume two servings of protein foods each day —
meat or eggs. Also include a variety of fruits and vegetables. Milk
and cheese, or foods made with milk, are vital as well.

A day on the trail which involves approximately seven hours
of walking requires about 3,500 calories and seventy grams of
protein. If you walk briskly, the totals are higher. You must seek
to maintain a balance between energy output and intake. Here is
a listing of the calorie and protein content of some trail foods:

Food	Calories (Ounces)	Protein Grams (Ounces)
Dried Beans	97	6.2
Oatmeal	110	4.0
Dried Apricots	86	1.5
Dried Prunes, Raisins	84	.6
Dried Potatoes	100	1.2
Margarine	205	.2
Cheddar Cheese	110	6.7
Dry Skimmed Milk	100	9.9
Peanut Butter	173	7.3
Dried Eggs	166	13.5
Sugar, Hard Candy	111	0
Milk Chocolate	152	1.6

The best reference book concerning the nutritional content of various foods is *Agricultural Handbook No. 8: Composition of Foods*, which is published by the U.S. Department of Agriculture. Almost two hundred pages in length, it consists mainly of two detailed tables, one titled, "Composition of Foods, 100 grams, edible portion," and the other, "Nutrients in the edible portion of 1 pound of food as purchased." The book is available in most public libraries, or you can order a copy from the Superintendent of Documents (U.S. Government Printing Office, Washington, D.C. 20402). It costs $1.50.

Food Purchasing

What foods you buy and in what quantity is an extremely subjective matter and the information set down in this section is meant to guide you in a general way. By investigation and trial and error you will arrive at a variety of meals and menus to suit your taste.

While nutritional value should be uppermost in your mind when shopping for freeze-dried foods, another important consideration is yield, or cooked weight. Read the fine print on the packet and ask yourself how many ounces of food will the contents produce. The ratio should be about one to five. A packet containing cheese omelette in freeze dried form and weighing 2.4 ounces should make for a completed meal weighing about twelve ounces. If the yield in ounces is not printed on the package, figure it out for yourself by adding to the package weight the weight of water that the directions specify (A standard measuring cup of water weighs 8 ounces).

It's revealing to compare packets in this regard. One processor offers a beef hash dinner which, according to the label, "serves four." The packet yields thirty-seven ounces. But with another processor, the four-serving packet yields forty-eight ounces.

Always read the label carefully as regards to the contents. Is the packet complete? Does the pancake mix contain egg and milk, or do you have to add these? Is there milk, sugar and salt in the hot cereal mix?

This brings up the matter of how long it should take to prepare a packet meal. Figure about twenty minutes of cooking time for each packet. Add to that, of course, the amount of time it's going to take you to build a fire or light your stove.

There are instant meals for backpackers on the market but be wary here. All you are supposed to do is add boiling water to the packet contents and wait four or five minutes. However, it's moot whether this type of processing is wholly successful with all kinds of food. My advice is to try out any truly "quickie" meal before your trip.

Finally, ask yourself whether the packet itself, that is, the manner in which the contents are packaged, is ecologically correct. Is the package material something that can be readily burned? Tinfoil is a problem. It won't burn; you can't bury it and expect it to decompose. You must either remove the foil wrapper before you enter the backcountry (several National Parks now make this mandatory) or carry the wrapping home for disposal.

Listed below are typical food packets, along with the weight in ounces, the yield in ounces, and the price of each. These packets are meant to provide two servings. Most are also available in servings for four. Usually the larger the packet, the lower the price per serving.

	Weight in Ounces	Yield in Ounces	Cost (Two Servings)
BREAKFAST FOODS			
Jiffy Cereal	3½	18	$ .42
Pancake Mix	5½	12	.44
French Toast	3	6	.49
(Syrup) Maple	4	4	.42
Scrambled Eggs	2¼	10	.92

Camp meals need no longer be commonplace, but read packets carefully.

	Weight in Ounces	Yield in Ounces	Cost (Two Servings)
BAKED GOODS AND SPREADS			
Biscuit Mix	7	12	.51
Grape Spred-Itt	1½	3	.27
Peanut Butter-Honey	2¼	3¾	.64
SOUP AND SALAD			
Chicken Noodle Soup	1½	20	.49
Lemon-Lime Veg. Gel Salad	1¾	9	.38
VEGETABLES			
Diced Carrots	1½	10	.47
Cream Corn	3	12	.96
Sweet Peas	2	6	.78
Peas'N Carrots	1½	8	.68
Peas'N Onions	3	8	1.12
Mexicali Corn	1½	10	.96
Diced Potatoes	3	16	.56
Mixed Veg. in Sauce	2	7	.70
Potatoes au Gratin	3	10	.74
DINNERS WITH MEAT			
Beef Hash	5	16	1.72
Beef Stew	5¾	20	1.74
Beef Stroganoff	7¾	24	1.72
Beef'N Gravy w/Noodles	6	30	1.73
Frontier Stew	5½	24	1.75
Chicken ala King	4	28	1.42
Chicken Noodle	6½	24	1.60
Veg-A-Rice Beef	5½	17	1.47
DINNERS, MEATLESS			
Boston Beans	6	14	.79
Macaroni'N Cheese	6	22	.82
Spaghetti-Tomato Sauce	5	18	.70
Veg-A-Rice (Chicken)	5	16	.68

	Weight in Ounces	Yield in Ounces	Cost (Two Servings)
DESSERTS			
Quik Rice Pudding	3½	10	.68
Vanilla Instant Pudding	3	10	.51
Cherry Cobbler	6	13	1.04
FRUITS			
Apple Sauce	2	9	.56
Stewed Apples	3	12	.96
Apricot Slices	2	6	.98
Fruit Mix	2	6	.70
Peach Slices	2	6	.83
BEVERAGES			
Tomato Juice	1	12	.50
Pink Lemonade	2½	25	.37
Sweet Milk Cocoa	4	25	.50

Besides food packets such as these, processors also sell tins of freeze-dried meats. For example, Chuck Wagon Foods, another of the larger firms, markets a small sealed can containing four freeze-dried beef steaks (three ounces, $3.75), and another containing four freeze-dried boneless pork chops (three and one-half ounces, $3.50). Kellogg's packages freeze-dried salad mixes in cans, tuna, crabmeat and chicken. Each rehydrates to six and one-half ounces of salad and costs about $3 a can.

With such a wide selection, it's easy to plan many different menus over a one- or two-week period. Breakfasts and lunches may be only one- or two-course meals, but with dinner you're likely to want to be much more indulgent. Begin the meal with tomato juice or a soup. As a main course, serve beef stroganoff (one of the most popular of hikers' meals) or a casserole-type dish like Veg-A-Rice Beef. For a side dish, pick out a vegetable pack or a salad, then fruit or pudding for dessert. There's even freeze-dried ice cream.

Of course, work out each day's menu before you depart. The backcountry is no place to do meal planning.

Cutting Food Costs

If you eat three meals a day of freeze-dried foods, your daily food cost is going to total $4 or $5. This may not seem unduly expensive for a weekend hike, but over an extended period, it can mount up. The alternative is to buy in bulk quantities.

For example, in planning breakfasts for a week-long hike, it's more economical to buy a bulk supply of dried eggs or cereal than seven different trail packets. Or a large package of dehydrated soup, the family size available at the supermarket, can be apportioned over several different lunches. Meat bars can serve as the basis for several dinners.

These are among the foods available in bulk quantities that get high ratings on the basis of nutritive value, light weight and ease of preparation.

EGGS   Dehydrated eggs are a staple item among backpackers. With most brands, one level tablespoon of powder, blended with two tablespoons of water or milk, is equivalent to one medium-size egg.

While the nutritive value of powdered eggs is high, since they are rich in vitamins A, B_1, G and minerals, the flavor leaves a bit to be desired, although manufacturers are continually improving the product. Trail veterans enhance the dish with bits of bacon, ham or cheese.

The U.S. Department of Agriculture uses powdered eggs by the ton in its various food distribution programs, and has available booklets containing recipes which feature the product. Write: Marketing and Consumer Services, U.S.D.A., Washington, D.C. 20250.

MEAT BARS   Read the label on a meat bar. You're likely to find these ingredients listed: dried lean meat, seedless raisins, dried apples, dextrose, peanuts, soy oil, hydrogenated shortening, vanilla extract and salt. Obviously, the idea is to pack as much nutrition as possible into a small package.

North American Indians made meat bars out of dried lean meat, which was pounded into a paste and mixed with fat and berries. They were known as pemmican, from the Cree word *pimi*, meaning fat or grease. The name isn't used any more, probably because modernday food processors feel that it suggests the primitive.

Modern meat bars are said to have about the same nutritive value as a pound of fresh beef. One bar can serve as a lunch, as a mid-afternoon pickup, or as the basis of the evening meal.

Besides eating the meat bar like a candy bar, you can prepare and serve it as ground meat. First crumble the bar, add onion or chili powder, allow it to stand for about ten minutes, then brown over a low flame while stirring. You can also add a crumbled bar to soup.

The three-ounce Campsite Meat Bar, which is made by Wilson's, is available at most camp equipment stores. It costs about 90¢. Uncooked its flavor is similar to cold beef hash. Wilson's also makes a Campsite Bacon Bar.

MILK Powdered white milk has a wide range of uses. A pound of it mixed with water makes a gallon. It serves as a drink by itself or can be used in the preparation of other dishes. Not only does it contain valuable fat, but also vitamins A, B_1, C, and minerals and protein — all of the nourishment of fresh milk.

Be sure to pack the powder in an airtight container. Otherwise it is likely to pick up odors. It will also take on moisture, which causes the powder to become lumpy.

One problem with powdered milk is that it sometimes dissolves slowly. You can overcome this by stirring the powder thoroughly before mixing.

Canned condensed milk is too bulky and heavy to consider, and most people find it less palatable than the powdered variety.

FRUIT JUICES, DRINKS Available in a tremendous assortment of flavors, powdered juices and fruit-ades are ideal for the backpacker. They can't be beaten in terms of convenience, and some, such as orange juice and grapefruit juice, get high marks for nutritive value.

Juices and drinks can be used to make unpalatable water most drinkable. Used creatively, they can give an added dimension to almost any meal. Lemon drink, for instance, is a treat with fresh-cooked trout.

SOUPS Like powdered juices and drinks, dehydrated soups are available in a great array. To make a soup meal a substantial one, cut by at least one-half the amount of water the recipe recommends. In other words, make a stew. A chunk of margarine will improve the flavor and increase the nutritive value of the dish.

FRUITS Most fruits stand up very well under the rigors of processing. They are useful as snacks or meal supplements. They are nutritious; they're flavorful.

Take dehydrated apples, for instance. They can be stewed and served as a side dish or dessert. They can be added to cooked or dry cereal. They can be used for making jam.

Dried prune and figs, stewed or eaten straight out of the box, have a mild laxative effect, and are a good item during the first day or so of your trip when your metabolism is adjusting to different water and new foods. They're rich in vitamins, too.

Peaches and apricots are full of flavor and vitamin rich as well. Apricots are an especially good source of vitamin C and thus can serve as a substitute for orange juice.

Raisins are splendid for nibbling as you walk along. Use them for quick energy or to stave off hunger pains in the hours before lunch or dinner.

Fruits are also available in bar form. Chuck Wagon Foods offers Mountain Bars — the Mt. Hood Bar (date and sesame seeds), the Mt. Rainier Bar (prune, apricot and walnuts) and the Mt. McKinley Bar (date, cherry, fig and almond). Each is compressed to about the size of a cigarette lighter, contains 160 calories and costs 39¢.

The same company offers fruit in sheet form. "Just unroll and tear off what you want," say the advertisements. In lemon, prune and apricot flavors, their "tear sheets," as they are called, are priced at 35¢ an ounce.

PREPARED BREAKFAST FOODS Most breakfast foods such as cornflakes don't have the substance or contain the nourishment to carry you for very many miles, but there are a couple of exceptions — Grape Nuts and All Bran. Either goes well with breakfast fruit or makes a tasty snack.

Oatmeal is a backpacker's standby. Be sure to get the instant kind.

VEGETABLES Beans, the traditional trail meal since the days of Daniel Boone, have given way to freeze-dried vegetables. They require too much space in the pack and take too long to cook. The same is true of split dried peas.

Not only do you have a large variety of vegetables from which to choose, but some of them can be prepared in different ways. Take potatoes, for instance. You can purchase them diced, julienne, mashed or hashed brown.

Dehydrated carrots are vitamin rich and a good source of iron. Be sure to pack them along if you're planning to do any nighttime hiking, for they help to overcome night blindness.

Sweet corn and green beans can be used as side dishes or in preparing stews. Tomatoes, onions and celery in flake form are excellent as flavorings.

Don't overlook dehydrated cabbage, a splendid source of vitamins A, B_1, C and G. Only eight ounces of the product is the equivalent of seven pounds of field cabbage.

MARGARINE   This is recommended over butter because of its superior keeping qualities. Use it in frying and put a dab of it in almost any vegetable dish to enhance flavor.

If you're making a particularly long summer trip, inquire at your local camp supply store about tropical butter. A tin of it will remain fresh for months and it is high in vitamin A.

CHEESE   A sharp, aged cheddar cheese is one of the most delectable of trail foods and is also useful in preparing a variety of main courses, such as egg dishes or any type of meal featuring pasta. Edam and Gouda are almost as versatile.

Heat makes cheese rubbery and on long trips it can become moldy. But there's a way to keep it fresh and tasty. Sew servings or cooking portions of the cheese in cheesecloth and then dip them in paraffin.

SPICES AND HERBS   Don't fail to take along small packets of pepper, oregano or garlic powder — or whatever appeals to you. Nutmeg and cinnamon are other possibilities. Paprika and powdered parsley improve flavor and add eye appeal. Other ideas will occur to you if you spend a few minutes at the spice counter of your local supermarket.

SUGAR   Concentrated-sugar substitutes may appeal to you because they represent less weight, but conventional granulated sugar is what is recommended. It's the best quick-energy food there is.

COFFEE AND TEA   Concentrated coffee, either instant or freeze-dried, is what most backpackers prefer but real coffee drinkers make trail coffee. Use two level tablespoons of coarsely ground coffee for each cup of water. Mix; set it on the fire. As soon as it boils, remove from the fire and let it brew for about five minutes. Settle the grounds with a tablespoon of cold water.

Coffee candy, which comes packaged like Life Savers, is another alternative. These are rich in flavor and contain caffeine.

Tea bags take up little space and less weight. Don't forget there's also powdered tea and that it comes in tablet form, too.

PEANUT BUTTER   A high energy food and very nourishing, peanut butter is excellent for between meal snacks. Supermarket peanut butter lacks the flavor of the freshly ground type, but one reason it does is because of the addition of preservatives that enhance its keeping qualities.

SALT   Keep in mind that you'll be perspiring more freely than usual, and must constantly replace the salt that you lose. Use extra table salt or, if the weather is extremely hot, take salt tablets, sold in drugstores.

Drawing from this list, a breakfast might consist of fruit juice, cereal with fruit, and coffee or tea, with plenty of sugar and milk. To boost the meal's protein content, an energy bar or part of a meat bar might be included.

Lunch could be made up of fruit juice or drink, cheese or peanut butter, and soup. Salad mix might also be included.

For dinner, a stew. It can consist of a meat bar, one or more packets of vegetables, plus herbs and spices for flavor. For dessert, serve fruit or prepare an instant pudding. You can vary the dinner menu by occasionally serving a freeze-dried steak or chops.

Prepacking Your Food

Don't pack along a sack of cereal, a jar of powdered fruit juice and the like. Prepack your food to get rid of outer wrappers and facilitate meal preparation.

Take small plastic bags and measure into them all of the items you need for an individual meal. For a breakfast, one bag might contain two teaspoons of instant coffee, two teaspoons of sugar, and two of powdered milk. Another bag would contain four ounces of dried cereal, raisins and several teaspoons of sugar. A third would have a teaspoon of powdered juice, while a fourth might contain an energy bar or a meat bar.

All of these would then be placed into a larger plastic bag which would be labeled "Breakfast," plus the day or date on which the meal is to be consumed. If you're planning a seven-day hike, you would have twenty-one such bags. Use a felt marking pen or a china marking pencil to write on plastic bags.

Water

How much water you will have to pack along depends on several factors. Most mountain trails lead past water occasionally, and so a canteenful at the start may be all that you need. But if you're heading into dry country, it's a different matter. You may have to carry all of your requirements. When you consider that one U.S. gallon weighs eight and one-third pounds, you get a clear understanding of the dimensions of the problem.

The other critical variable is the amount of water that you consume under ordinary circumstances. No two people are alike in this regard. Some people get along nicely on a glass or two a day, while others require more than a quart. What this means is that you will have to work out for yourself how much water to take.

If the supply of water is limited, it is better to drink frequently and sparingly than to try to restrain yourself to the point of discomfort. At each rest stop, take a few sips. Rinse the water around in your mouth before you swallow it. If you wait too long to drink, you'll gulp down larger amounts.

Your best source of water is snow. Rainwater, which can be collected by spreading out a poncho or other waterproof fabric so that it drains into a container, is safe, too. You can also collect rainfall from cavities in rock formations, so long as the rain is of recent vintage.

Most other water has to be considered unfit to drink, no matter how clear it appears. An exception may be a mountain spring that bubbles up from live rock or clean soil, and is not near any contaminating influence. But the rule you must follow is this: "When in doubt, purify." — and you should almost always be in doubt.

Fifteen minutes of boiling renders any water safe. But what you end up with is a scorching drink. It can hardly be called a thirst quencher on a summer afternoon, or even on a winter's afternoon, and the whole process is very time consuming.

A better way is to purify by means of Halazone, which chlorinates the water. All you do is fill your canteen, drop in a tablet (one for each pint you're purifying), screw on the top and

(Oasis)

(Palco)

Canteens are traditionally of cloth-covered aluminum.

Newer canteens take the form of polyethylene flasks.▶

wait for half an hour. If you want to overcome the taste of chlorine, add some powdered fruit drink mix.

Halazone tablets can be obtained at any drugstore. They cost not much more than a penny apiece.

Iodine tablets can be used to purify water, too. Lacking tablets, you can also use three drops of 2 percent iodine per quart of water. Wait thirty minutes before drinking.

Canteens

The traditional canteen is a steel or aluminum container shaped like a large pocket watch. A heavy cloth cover protects the metal and keeps the water cool. (When the cloth is wetted and the canteen put in the sun, evaporation cools the water inside.) Canteens are available in one-, two- and four-quart sizes.

Many of today's backpackers prefer to use screw-top polyethylene bottles to carry water. These come in a variety of sizes and are much lighter in weight and inexpensive. They are proving so popular that some canteen manufacturers have added them to their product line.

(*Oasis*)

Living Off the Land

If you have visions of entering an unmapped wilderness area and using your equipment plus the available gifts of nature to see you through, you're romanticizing. An experienced and knowledgeable expert on woodcraft and nature lore could manage to survive for an indefinite period under such circumstances without outside help, but for the average person the experience is likely to prove wearisome, if not tragic. Just about every waking minute would have to be spent searching for food. By taking the foods you require, you're better able to use your time relishing the sights and sounds about you.

You can, however, supplement your food supply with what nature offers. Strawberries, blackberries and blueberries may be available for the plucking. A mountain stream may provide a breakfast trout.

There is more, sometimes much more, but you have to be able to perceive it. Oval-shaped plantain leaves are somewhat similar to lettuce, but are crunchier and have a distinctive flavor. The petals of wild daisies are perfectly edible, but avoid the yellow center.

Dandelion greens can be nibbled on, too. Because of the danger of insecticides, they should be picked at least ten feet from the road.

During summer hikes, you may come upon mature ferns. By pulling firmly at the base, you will bring up a banana-shaped shoot (leaving the root intact). It's gray on the ouside and yellow inside. Peeled and eaten raw, these taste like almonds.

Mushrooms? Don't take a chance. Even the experts pass them by.

Wood sorrel, which can be recognized by its leaves shaped like canoe paddles, adds zest to packaged soups. The tips of young spicebush twigs can be used for making an aromatic tea.

If you're interested in learning more about nature's foods, these books are recommended; *Free for the Eating*, by Bradford Angier (Stackpole Co., 1966, $4.95); *Wild Edible Plants of the Western U.S.*, by Vinson Brown (Naturegraph, 1970, $3.95); and *The Ranger's Guide to Useful Plants of the Eastern Wilds*, by an American Indian, Deganawidah (Christopher Publishing, 1964, $3).

A leading guidebook to harmful plants is *Deadly Harvest*, by John M. Kingsbury (Holt, Rinehart & Winston, 1966, $4.50).

CHAPTER SIX
Trail Cookery

Cooking over an open fire has always been considered one of the chief joys of camping. But small cook-stoves are now being used more and more on wilderness trails, and even the staunchest of traditionalists praise them.

The basic reason for their popularity is efficiency. You can boil a pint of water in five or six minutes. Or you can prepare a cup of coffee in your tent in bad weather. There's no need to hunt up fuel. There's no time spent coaxing the fire to start, a chore that can take up the better part of a drizzly evening. Furthermore, there are no lengthy clean-up chores as with fire.

Weight and bulk used to be the chief shortcomings of stoves. But these aren't real problems any more. A modern portable cooking unit doesn't weigh any more than a day's supply of food and takes up about the same amount of space.

Stoves do have one serious drawback. There is no recorded instance of anyone developing a romantic or even enthusiastic attachment for a stove on the basis of esthetics. A campfire, however, gets many points on this score.

To many backpackers, the campfire is as much a part of wilderness travel as blue sky and solitude.
(*U.S.D.A. Forest Service; Jim Hughes*)

But no one is saying you can't have a campfire — too — and that's what backpackers are doing. They're taking along a stove for cooking, but they build a fire in the evening, a traditional campfire. They are thus having the best of both worlds.

The Open Fire

To build an open fire quickly and efficiently, the kindling is the key. The best source of small dried sticks — the largest should not be any bigger in diameter than your thumb — are the dead lower branches of pine, spruce, cedar and other evergreens. This is sometimes referred to as squaw wood because Indian women gathered it. A standing dead tree may supply you with all the wood you need, both kindling and the heavier stuff.

If it has been raining and everything is soaked, take a length of heavy firewood and split smaller pieces out of the center to use as kindling. A standard woodsman's method is to make a fire stick, or a fuzz stick. Using a knife or hatchet, shave long strips on one end of a stick of dead wood, until you have what looks like a miniature pine tree. A pair of these propped against each other with a few shavings beneath will start burning at the touch of a match. An easier method is to use a candle or a tube of barbecue igniter paste.

Before you lay your kindling, clear an area up to six feet in diameter, digging down to reach the bare earth. Never build a fire on humus or pine needles. Be sure there are no bushes nearby or any overhanging branches.

Arrange the kindling as if you were building a small teepee, with the sticks leaning against each other at the top. Fire at the bottom, carefully shielding the flame for the first minute or so.

Have plenty of heavier wood close by, adding it as soon as the pyramid is burning well. Different woods burn differently. If you plan to do all of your cooking over open fires, you should learn to recognize the trees best suited for firewood. Here is how some common woods rate on the basis of combustibility:

Good	*Fair*	*Poor*
Ash	Beech	Alder
Dogwood	Tamarack	Magnolia
Oak	Sycamore	Willow
Birch	Cedar	Chestnut
Maple	Pine	Catalpa
Hickory	Juniper	Cherry
Holly	Fir	White Elm
Apple	Spruce	
Locust	Cottonwood	
	Aspen	

Always be apprehensive about your fire and its potential for destruction. Whenever possible, lay a ring of stones around the fire to reduce the chances of its spreading. Never leave a fire unattended.

Don't make the mistake of merely putting out the fire. Soak the embers with water or, if none is available, smother them with dirt. When you think that you've accomplished your task, repeat the process. "Kill your fire dead," is what the U.S. Forest Service instructs.

Stones can be used to support your grate or cookpots.
(Oregon Freeze Dried Foods)

If you're simply going to boil some water, arrange three or four stones to support the cooking pot and build the fire within and around these. When there are no stones available, make what is known as a hunter's fire. Place two logs side by side, a few inches apart. Build the fire between the logs and rest the pot on top.

Another method, one that requires a larger fire, involves a pair of forked sticks and crossbar cut from a straight-growing limb or tree. The forked sticks are planted into the ground a few feet apart and the fire is built in between. The cooking pot hangs from the crossbar which is suspended between the sticks. Use green wood and splash water on the sticks from time to time.

Still another method is to dig a trench parallel to the prevailing wind. Build the fire in the trench and set the pot across the top.

On a very windy day, try this: Dig a hole slightly larger than the pot and about two-feet deep. Build the fire on the bottom. When it's burning vigorously, suspend the pot on a stick laid across the mouth of the hole. This conserves fuel and prevents the wind from blowing the fuel away.

You may want to consider buying a metal grate, especially if you are going to be hiking in an area where stones and sticks are in limited supply. One type of grate that is splendid for back-packing features stainless steel tubing, is five inches by fifteen inches in size, and weighs only three ounces.

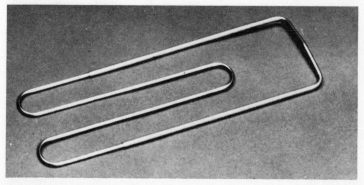

A backpacker's grate.
(*Gerry Division; Outdoor Sports Industries*)

Stoves for Backpackers

"Ten years ago I bought a small gas-burning stove for use in a fuelless mountain area above timberline, and the stove turned out to be so efficient that I have virtually given up open-fire cooking." Colin Fletcher makes this statement in *The Complete Walker* (published by Alfred A. Knopf), and he is enough of an expert so that his endorsement of gas-stove cookery has to be taken very seriously.

Even where good firewood is in plentiful supply, a stove offers several distinct advantages over an open fire, and under certain conditions, a stove is the only way to cook.

There is no time spent in rummaging for wood and fussing with the fire. You have complete control over the heat source, a benefit that you will be quick to recognize if you've ever tried to pan-fry on a windy day.

Stoves are usually classified according to the type of fuel they use, which can be alcohol, kerosene, gasoline or gas (butane or propane). Make your evaluation of stoves on the basis of weight (including fuel and fuel containers), ease of use, fuel capacity, burning time per unit of fuel, sturdiness of construction, stability (once placed on the ground) and cost.

A small alcohol-burning pocket stove, only three inches across, lights instantly and can boil water in five minutes. It weighs about eight ounces and costs less than $3.

Sterno heaters burn solidified alcohol. They may be unsophisticated but they're rugged and economical. A seven-ounce can of Sterno costs less than $1. It cannot spill because it's solid and burns right in the can in which it is packed. The Sterno stove folds flat and weighs only a few ounces.

The Coleman Company, Inc. (Wichita, Kansas 67201), the country's leading manufacturer of gasoline stoves, offers backpackers a single-burner unit, only five and one-half inches in diameter and weighing less than three pounds. Called the Sportster, it comes with a variety of accessories including a combination carrying case and cook kit.

When gasoline, kerosene or alcohol is used as stove fuel, it has to be converted into a gas for burning. This is done in a part of the stove known as the generator unit. The conversion requires large amounts of air plus proper pressure inside the fuel tank in one's hand, which expands the air inside and forces a few drops of fuel out of a tiny hole in the burner unit. This is

The Sportster.
(*Coleman*)

then lighted with a match. Once ignited, the burner continues to draw from the fuel reservoir.

In larger gasoline stoves, pressure has to be maintained while the stove is in use by means of a built-in hand pump. Any time the blue flames seem to be diminishing in size or intensity, air must be pumped into the tank.

However, a number of Swedish-made gas-burning stoves, inexpensive and light in weight, do not require hand-pumping. (It is a stove of this type that received Colin Fletcher's glowing praise.) Optimus, Inc., (P.O. Box 3848, 652 East Commonwealth, Fullerton, Calif. 92634) is the leading manufacturer of these stoves.

Such stoves burn white gas or the special appliance fuel sold in sporting goods stores. (Standard automobile gasoline, if it contains lead which can clog the stove fuel lines, should be used only in an emergency.) Spare gas can be carried in aluminum bottles with leak-proof screwtops.

To light one of the Swedish-made stoves, you first open the fuel control valve, and then warm the bowl in your hands or by placing the unit in the sun. This forces a small amount of liquid fuel to collect in a depression at the base of the generator. When you ignite this, it heats the generator and vaporizes some fuel. Then you can light the stove. The heat of burning maintains pressure upon the fuel. In other words, no hand-pumping is necessary.

Carry fuel in aluminum bottles like these.
(Camp & Trail Outfitters)

Optimus Stoves

Optimus manufactures and markets dozens of different types of stoves for campers and boatmen, but there are three in particular that backpackers prefer. The Svea, a gleaming brass and aluminum cylinder unit, is the most compact and lightest of the three, less than five inches in diameter and five inches deep. Its top cover serves as a small cooking pot. The Svea weighs a mere one and one-half pounds, yet it can boil an egg in six minutes. Its list price is $14.95.

While the Svea is the most compact of the Optimus stoves, the 111B is the most efficient and versatile. Roughly seven inches square, four inches deep, weighing three and one-half pounds, it will boil a quart of water in about four minutes. And it will do it at just about any altitude and at temperatures ranging from 90°F to −40°F. Its fuel tank has a one-pint capacity, which provides a burning time of about two hours. The 111B lists at $23.95.

The third stove, the Optimus 8R, is a scaled down version of the 111B. This, too, is roughly square shaped (5″ × 5″ × 3″). It weighs one and one-half pounds and lists at $15.95. It operates with much the same efficiency as the Svea, boiling a quart of water in six to seven minutes. Its fuel tank holds one-third pint of fuel, giving a burning time of one and one-quarter hours.

The Svea; its cover is a cooking pot.
(*Optimus*)

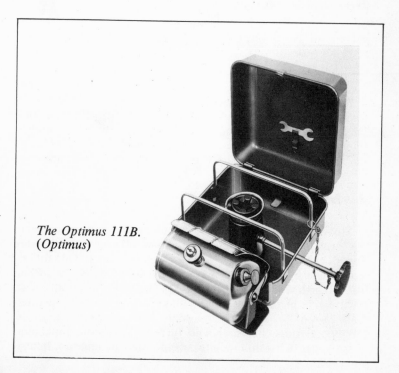

The Optimus 111B.
(*Optimus*)

The Optimus 8R.
(*Optimus*)

"Our gasoline stoves are most popular among backpackers," says Bengt O. Frieberg, President of Optimus, "but we have lately found an increased demand for our kerosene models. Quite a few people in the Southwest go backpacking in Mexico and kerosene is more readily available there than gasoline . . ."

Using Bottled Fuel

Stoves that use butane or propane as a fuel take longer to boil water than gas stoves, but in some other aspects they are superior. They are cleaner. They are light in weight. One folding type made by the Primus-Sievert Company (354 Sackett Point Rd., North Haven, Conn. 06473), with its disposable fuel cartridge in place, takes up about as much space as a one-quart milk carton.

One cartridge holds enough fuel for two and one-half to three hours of use and weighs three quarters of a pound. It costs less than $1. When using fuel of this type, there's no need to pre-heat, and, of course, there's no hand-pumping.

These stoves weigh slightly more than one pound. They cost approximately $10, or slightly less.

When using a butane or propane fueled stove, you have to be careful to shield it from the wind. Most models now come equipped with cleverly designed windshields. Even so, on a windy day you should check the flame occasionally to be sure that it is still burning.

This propane cookstove costs less than $10. (Winchester)

The units are made so that fuel-cartridge fittings can be tightened sufficiently by hand when being installed. If a connection turns hard, check for cross threading. Don't force it.

If you suspect a leak, for obvious reasons don't test with a lighted match. Apply soapy water to the suspected area and watch for bubbles.

In pelting rain or extreme cold, you may want to prepare a meal or perhaps a warming drink inside your tent. You can do this using the stoves described in this section, but you have to exercise caution.

If it is at all possible, set up the stove outside the tent and fire it before you bring it inside. Have the food ready to cook.

Burning gasoline will use up oxygen quickly in a closed area and create carbon monoxide in its place. It is colorless, odorless — and lethal. Keeping the tent well ventilated, with fresh air sweeping through, is the way to guard against carbon monoxide poisoning.

No matter what type of stove you decide upon, follow the manufacturers operating instructions to the letter. Be sure to add the words "stove instruction booklet" to your equipment checklist.

Called the "Mini Stove," this unit weighs only seven ounces.

High Altitude Cookery

The higher you climb, the longer it will take you to cook up a meal that requires boiling water. This is because the temperature required to boil water falls 1° Centigrade with every 1,000-foot increase in elevation. At sea level, water boils at 100° Centigrade; at 5,000 feet, it boils at 95° Centigrade.

You probably won't notice much of a difference unless you're ascending some of the higher Rocky Mountain peaks. If you ever want to raise the boiling point of water, simply add a pinch or two of salt.

Cooking and Eating Utensils

Virtually all camping equipment dealers feature elaborate cooking kits. These are suitable for a weekend hike but for an extended trip you should be very discerning in your choice of cooking equipment and eating utensils. The paragraphs that follow appraise the basic items you will need.

FRYING PAN Stainless steel, not aluminum, is recommended. Food is more likely to stick to an aluminum pan, especially if you're going to be cooking on an open fire. A steel pan is also better because it spreads the heat more evenly and retains it better. Your frying pan doesn't have to be more than ten inches in diameter. It should be equipped with a folding or detachable handle. Remember, it's your dinner plate, too.

COOKING POTS You'll need two of these, the larger holding no more than two quarts. They should be made of aluminum and each should have a snug-fitting cover. Be sure that the bail handles lock firmly in an upright position so the kettles can be hung over the fire.

Light fabric covers can be purchased for the frying pan and cooking pots to permit you to pack them without scouring off the black char that may accumulate. These are a bit redundant, however. It is a fact that some blackness makes for a more even spread of heat. When you return home, you can give aluminum cookwear a thorough cleaning by using a solution made by dissolving a tablespoon of cream of tartar in a pint of water.

Cooking and eating utensils should nest into a single unit.
(*Palco*)

DRINKING CUPS Stainless steel makes an excellent cup.
Aluminum does, too, but since it is overly efficient in conducting
heat you may burn your lips on the rim when trying to consume
a hot drink or soup. Be sure the cup handle is mounted and constructed in such a way that it will stay cool. Tough plastic cups
are also suitable.

SPOON You need a spoon, either aluminum or steel, but
consider a fork to be something of a luxury.

KNIFE U.S. Forest Rangers claim to be able to judge a backpacker by the type of sheath knife he wears. A novice in the
woods is almost certain to be wearing something that resembles
a bowie knife, the blade at least twelve inches in length. Such a
weapon probably was useful to Bowie himself in defending The
Alamo, but it is not of great value to the woodsman.

A knife with a four-to six-inch blade should be enough for
all your camping needs. High quality steel is a must but stainless
steel isn't. Blades of stainless steel are difficult to resharpen. Get
a blade that is heavy enough so that it will not bend.

Beware of gimmicky handles, those with finger grips or other
and similar features. Look for a simple handle made of antler,
wood or laminated leather discs. Examine the knife carefully to
be sure the blade and handle are securely joined.

The sheath is often a clue to a knife's quality or lack of it. It should be made of sturdy oil-tanned leather with stout stitching along the outer edge. Be sure it has a strip of leather that snaps around the handle, called a keep lock.

Stay away from knives that are decked out with a multitude of gadgets. Every sports equipment store features several of these. Besides a cutting blade, a knife of this type will feature a nail file, bottle opener, can opener, screw driver, scissors, etc., etc. Ask to look at one because they are quite fascinating from a mechanical standpoint. But it's wholly impractical to own one.

SHARPENING STONE Take along a carborundum whetstone to keep the knife sharp. There are types especially for backpacking which measure about three inches in length. There are others not too much larger than a paper match but these are too small to be considered practical.

SALT AND PEPPER SHAKER Look for the twin-compartment metal or plastic shaker. Most sporting goods stores have them. Clear plastic is the best because you can see how much is left.

FOOD CONTAINERS Even if you prepack all your meals, you will still need to pack along several food containers. Sugar and margarine should be carried in containers of polyethelene, which is both strong and light. Detergent can be carried in such a container, too. Select containers of distinctive sizes so you won't be putting detergent into your morning coffee.

CAN OPENER The standard GI can opener, which has the general dimensions of a large paper clip and about the same weight (it weighs one-eighth of an ounce, actually), is what to buy if you're packing along canned goods. They're available at most Army surplus stores, although some sporting goods stores now stock them.

MATCHSAFE Made of plastic or metal, this is a small cylinder-shaped case with a screwtop that holds twenty or so wooden kitchen matches.

Incidentally, matches can be rendered waterproof by dipping the heads in paraffin or nail polish. There's no law that says you can't take along book matches, although most woodsmen

A metal matchsafe.
(*National Park Service;
Photo Fred E. Mang, Jr.*)

seem to shun them. Keep them in a plastic bag so they won't be
a problem in wet weather.

REFLECTOR OVEN   The reflector oven has been used suc-
cessfully since pioneer days to bake bread and biscuits and even
roast fish and meat, but it's not something you're going to be
able to utilize unless you're planning open-fire cookery. The
oven is made of lightweight sheet aluminum and is boxlike in
shape. When placed eight to ten inches from the fire, the oven's
angled top and bottom direct the heat toward a central shelf
which supports the bread dough. Biscuits can be baked in about
twenty minutes.

The oven folds flat so that it can be carried without great
difficulty. Weight is a more serious problem than bulk. A reflector oven weighs about $2\frac{1}{2}$ pounds.

Using a reflector oven also presupposes that you are going to
pack along flour, baking powder, extra salt and the other ingredients and the utensils your recipes require.

DUTCH OVEN   The Dutch oven is also used for baking outdoors but the principle is different. Essentially a large kettle
made of aluminum (they used to be cast iron) with a tight-
fitting lid, the oven is buried in hot ashes and coals and more
coals are heaped over the cover. In the days before dried and
dehydrated foods, Dutch ovens were frequently used to brew
stews and bake bread, but they have pretty much gone the way
of bannock and jerked beef.

Foil Cookery

Aluminum foil can be a valuable aid to the outdoor cook. You can use it to wrap meats, fish and some vegetables, place the packet in the fire or on it, and the result is a succulent dish.

The foil also does away with the need to carry cooking utensils. Simply press it into the shape of a pot or shallow pan, using enough layers to give the container sufficient stiffness. To bake bread, corn bread or biscuits, place the dough in the center of a long strip of foil, fold the foil over, allowing space for the dough to rise. Place on hot coals. Bread bakes in about fifteen minutes if the foil is surrounded by glowing coals.

A good fire is the key to successful foil cookery. With hardwood, allow at least forty minutes for the fire to burn down to the coals; softwood won't require so much time.

If you want more information on foil cookery, including menus and recipes, write: Home Economics Department, Reynolds Metals Co., 19 East 47th St., New York, N.Y. 10017.

Campfire Cookery

To some backpackers, a minority to be sure, freeze-dried foods rank with city air and highway billboards as evidence of the nation's decline. They cherish the traditional methods of camp cooking, or, at least, blend them with the new. It is for these campers that these recipes, all tried and proven, are given.

JOHNNYCAKE

Also known as corncake, this bread is made of cornmeal and cooked in a frying pan or baked in a foil packet.

1 cup yellow cornmeal	$\frac{1}{4}$ cup reconstituted powdered milk
$\frac{1}{2}$ cup flour	2 tablespoons powdered eggs
1 teaspoon baking powder	2 tablespoons shortening or margarine
$\frac{1}{2}$ teaspoon salt	
	grease

Mix cornmeal, flour, baking powder and salt. Add milk, powdered eggs and shortening or margarine. Spread batter in a greased frying pan and tilt the pan almost upright, facing the fire; or shape the batter into a loaf for baking in foil.

FRENCH TOAST

8 slices of bread	salt
6 tablespoons powdered eggs	pepper
6 tablespoons water	grease
12 tablespoons reconstituted powdered milk	

Mix powdered eggs, water and milk, and season with salt and pepper. Dip bread into batter, and fry in a lightly greased pan until crisp.

OMELET (FOR TWO)

You'll need a spatula for this recipe.

6 tablespoons powdered eggs	pepper
2 tablespoons reconstituted powdered milk	grease
16 tablespoons water (1 cup)	filling — onions,
salt	mushrooms or bacon bits (optional)

Mix powdered eggs, milk and water. Add pinches of salt and pepper. Beat. Pour batter into a lightly greased, thoroughly heated frying pan, tilting the pan so that the batter covers the sides. Add filling, if desired. When brown underneath, use spatula to fold over. Turn and brown before serving.

RANGER'S HASH (SERVES FOUR)

1 package dehydrated potatoes	salt
water	pepper
1 teaspoonful freeze-dried onions	other seasonings (to taste)
1 packet freeze-dried carrots	1 can (12 ounces) corned beef
	grease

Put package of dehydrated potatoes into a saucepan and cover with water. Let stand until fully hydrated. Cover with water again and boil for ten minutes (with lid on). Add freeze-dried onions and carrots, salt, pepper and other seasonings. Last, add corned beef, and mash with a fork.

Grease frying pan, and cook hash until brown on bottom. Then turn, and brown on the other side.

FRYING PAN BREAD (BANNOCK)

3 cups flour
½ teaspoon salt
1 tablespoon baking powder

1 cup reconstituted powdered milk, or water
2 tablespoons bacon drippings

Mix flour, salt and baking powder. Add milk or water, and stir in bacon drippings. Form into a loaf. Put pan on fire until loaf sets and begins to brown on bottom. Then tilt the pan to catch the reflected heat.

PAN-BROILED TROUT

1 small trout
milk
flour (or equal parts flour and corn-meal)

salt
pepper
2 tablespoons bacon fat or margarine

Clean small trout by removing entrails and gills only. Wipe and dip into milk, then into flour (or cornmeal and flour) to which salt and pepper have been added. Put bacon fat or margarine into a hot frying pan and drop the trout in, turning only after well browned on one side. For trout up to ten inches in length, four or five minutes of cooking time is sufficient — do not overcook. For a larger trout, allow more time, and cut into chunks for thorough cooking.

CAMP-FRIED POTATOES

¼ pound bacon
2 large onions
6 medium-sized potatoes
celery salt

powdered garlic
salt
pepper

Dice bacon into a frying pan. Fry until crisp. Slice onions, and cook until soft. Peel potatoes, and slice them into pan. Season. Cover, and cook until potatoes are soft. Remove cover. Increase heat, turning potatoes until they are tender and well browned.

FISH CHOWDER

Any type of freshly caught fish can be used in this recipe, and the more kinds the better.

fish	2 large onions
water	4 large potatoes
2 ounces vinegar	oregano
pickling spices	thyme
salt	1 can evaporated milk
pepper	1 lump butter or margarine
$\frac{1}{4}$ pound salt pork	1 tablespoon paprika

Take the fish as it comes from the water, and remove entrails and gills; leave scales, fins and head on the fish. Wash thoroughly, and cut into three-inch lengths. Place in a good-sized pot with enough water to cover fish. Add vinegar, a pinch of pickling spice and salt and pepper. Poach fish gently for about fifteen minutes, then remove from heat.

Meanwhile, dice salt pork into frying pan, and slice in onions. Allow them to cook until they are soft.

Strain the water in which the fish was cooked, and put liquid back into original pot. Allow fish to cool. Peel and dice potatoes, and add to fish liquid. Cook the potatoes until they are soft.

Add a pinch of oregano, thyme and pepper to the salt pork and onions, allowing a few minutes for the heat to bring out the flavor.

When the fish is cool, peel off skin, and remove bones. Add fish to cooked potatoes, and simmer. Pour milk into the pan with the salt pork and onions. When heated thoroughly — but not boiling — add to fish and potatoes. Add butter or margarine and paprika. Allow to stand so that the flavors will blend.

POPCORN Around the campfire, popcorn can be a treat. Cook it in a covered aluminum saucepan or a frying pan covered with aluminum foil.

Back-Country Housekeeping

Carry along a supply of detergent in a plastic bottle. After a meal, wash all the utensils that need washing, if you have enough water. If not, wait until you come to a brook or stream.

Soap or detergents should be used in a pan, not put into lakes or streams, because of the harm that they can do to aquatic life along the shore. Try to dispose of wash water in a rocky area where drainage will not endanger plant life.

Burn whatever garbage is burnable. For environmental reasons, carry out cans, bottles, aluminum foil and whatever else will not burn. Cans are easier to carry if they are flattened. A small plastic bag is ideal as a litterbag.

Don't bury your noncombustibles. Some years ago the National Park Service instituted trash-burying at Yosemite and they almost turned it into the world's largest garbage dump. "Pack in, pack out" is the policy now.

CHAPTER SEVEN

Camping Overnight; Sleeping Bags and Tents

Your sleeping bag will probably be the single most expensive piece of equipment you will purchase. But don't try to pinch pennies here. The sleeping bag is a basic requirement for your enjoyment and the right type of bag, properly cared for, is likely to last you for as long as you camp.

The idea of the sleeping bag, of course, is to keep you warm, but it does not produce warmth itself. It is simply meant to prevent the heat produced by your body from escaping into the open air. Succinctly, it insulates.

Fill Materials

Efficiency of insulation relates directly to thickness. Any material that keeps the air in the core of the bag from circulating will be effective insulation. Two inches of steel wool or shredded newspaper will keep you just as warm as two inches of prime goose down.

A quality sleeping bag is more important to your comfort and enjoyment than well-fitting boots.
(National Park Service Photo; Fred E. Mang, Jr.)

But outdoor experts recommend down bags to the exclusion of all others, and they are the most popular type by far. This isn't difficult to understand. Down, the fine, fluffy quill-less material that underlies a bird's outer contour of feathers, is number one because of its light weight, compressibility and resilience. A single ounce of high quality down will fill five hundred to six hundred cubic inches, yet can be compressed to about fifteen cubic inches for packing and carrying. Such a bag will weigh less than five pounds.

Down has other miraculous qualities. It breathes, allowing moisture in the form of perspiration (produced at the rate of one pint every eight hours) to pass through the bag. Otherwise, you'd wake up a clammy mess. Down is also soft and odorless.

Most experts agree that prime northern goose down makes for the very best filler. If, for reasons of economy, you choose prime duck instead, you will get only 80- to 85- percent efficiency as compared to goose down.

Never make a judgment about a sleeping bag based upon how much down the bag contains, measured in ounces. Remember what was said earlier in this section, that warmth relates to thickness of insulation. Once a bag contains sufficient down to deaden air circulation, cramming more down in won't increase warmth.

You want down that has good loft, or fluffiness. And there has to be an evenness to the loft, or air pockets might form.

Dacron is also commonly used as a fill material, but it is not much more than adequate. Dacron bags are all right if you have a mule hauling your equipment or you're automobile camping, but for backpacking the material gets a low rating as far as both bulk and weight are concerned. Dacron also has a tendency to ball up in corners of the bag, so extra stitching is necessary to keep it in place.

How much thickness should your bag have? It depends on the temperatures you're going to encounter. The U.S. Army Quartermaster Corps uses this data as a guide:

	Temperature			
	40°F	20°F	0°F	−0°F
Insulation thickness	$1\frac{1}{2}''$	$2''$	$2\frac{1}{2}''$	$3''$

Buy your bag for the coldest temperature you expect — naturally.

Called the "Wilderness Sleeper," this bag provides comfort to temperatures that range as low as 0°F.
(Gerry Division; Outdoor Sports Industries)

Bag Shape

This topic is almost as critical as the matter of fill. The shape of the bag should conform closely to your body shape. This means that you should buy a tapered, "mummy" bag.

The mummy bag, with its drawstring hood, allows you to enclose yourself almost completely, and this is regarded as significant advance over the old, rectangular bags, which failed to provide sufficient protection for the shoulders and none at all for the head. In addition, the rectangular bag's wide mouth allowed body heat to escape, thus sharply reducing the bag's effectiveness.

Construction

Once you have found a down-filled mummy bag that seems suitable, the next thing to check is the way in which it has been put together. To prevent the down from shifting and leaving spots where there is no insulation, just layers of thin shell, the bag is divided into a series of parallel tubes and each tube is further divided by partitions, or baffles.

First check the direction in which the tube stitching runs. With a quality bag, it will run horizontally. Tube stitching which runs vertically isn't nearly as good.

Next, check the baffle design and shape by holding the bag up to the light. It is likely to be one of three types (see diagram). The simply box-baffle is what to avoid. There is no insulating protection at the stitch points and cold spots can develop as a result.

The slant-box baffle is much more efficient. Its offset construction serves to hold the down in place, and because the stitch points in the upper and lower walls do not join you don't have to worry about cold spots developing.

Truss construction is the best of all. Down is held securely in place and there are no stitched-through areas.

The better bags also employ a differential cut, which means that the interior fabric is cut to a smaller circumference than the exterior fabric. Differential cutting allows the down to loft properly and prevents the outside shell from compressing upon the inside one when the inside bag is spread out. Equally important, differential cutting will not allow a cold spot to develop should you, the sleeper, poke out a knee or elbow. To check for

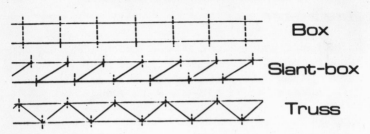

differential cut, spread out the inside of the bag to its fullest length; the outside should remain perfectly limp.

Opposed to the differential cut is what is called a space-filler cut, one in which both the inner and outer fabrics are cut to the same circumference. This is not entirely bad, so long as you are a quiet sleeper.

As for the fabric itself, ripstop nylon is now very much in vogue among backpackers. It is light in weight, resists abrasions and has a tear-strength that is two or three times greater than other fabrics of similar weight. The bag should be stitched with a polyester-core thread which has an exterior cotton wrapping. This type of thread is not only extremely strong and durable, but the cotton serves to fill the holes made by the needle as each stitch is taken.

How much will a bag that has all these features cost? It depends on how much warmth you are going to require and how good a shopper you are. But any quality mummy bag, with $2\frac{1}{2}$ pounds of prime down, about the amount you will need, and with the other features recommended here, will cost anywhere from $60 to $75, and better models range to $125.

Size

Sleeping bags are described as being of cut size or finished size. Cut size refers to the dimensions of the bag's cover before stitching. Finished size is the completed size, after all the sewing is done. This is what concerns you.

It is not likely that the size of the bag will be any problem unless you are at least six-feet tall. Then you'll have to order what some manufacturers call an X-long type, which is six feet, six inches in length. It increases the cost by about 10 percent and the weight by about four ounces.

Pick out a tapered down-filled bag with horizontal stitching.
(Sierra Designs)

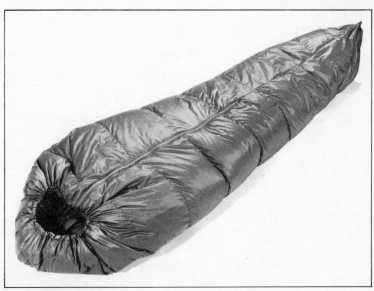

This mummy bag covers the head completely and, by means of a drawstring, pulls tight about the face.
(Jones Tent and Awning Ltd.)

A double mummy bag.
(Sierra Designs)

Bag zippers should be the heavy duty type.
(National Park Service Photo; Fred E. Mang, Jr.)

Be sure the bag has an overall tapered cut, being widest at the shoulders and slimmest at the ankles, and then widening again to accommodate the feet.

Mummy bags are easy enough to get into and out of, but some are fitted with zippers on one side to facilitate entry and exit. Don't consider a zipper a necessity. It adds to the bag cost and to its weight, and, unless it has an efficient overlap, can allow warm air to leak to the outside. One supposed advantage of the zipper is that it allows the bag to be partially opened in warm weather for cooling, but with bags of the nonzipper type all you have to do is remove the hood and open the top to achieve the same effect.

If you do want a zipper, get one of heavy-duty plastic; metal conducts cold. It should be the double-pull type, so that you can open the bag from either the top or bottom.

Mummy bags can be ordered in pairs with the zippers on opposite sides so that the bags can be joined. Zippers can be installed at cost of about $5 each. Furthermore, there are double mummy bags.

Selecting a Campsite

When you are ready to spread out your sleeping bag, the most important feature to look for is level ground. If there is even the slightest sideways slope, or if your feet are going to be slanted higher than your head, or vice versa, you are sure to be in for an uncomfortable night. Should you be camping on sloping land, such as a hillside, seek out ground around a large tree or scrape away enough topsoil to create a level grade.

Getting shelter from the wind is next in importance. A clump of bushes, a large tree or a rock wall will help. Shelter from the rain is discussed in the section that follows.

Ground Cover

A sleeping bag on the bare ground will not provide you with the comfort necessary for a good night's sleep. You need something to insulate your head, shoulders and back from the cold and dampness of the ground.

Up until fairly recent times, the average backpacker solved this problem by cutting limbs from live trees and making a bough bed. Or he piled up leaves, grass or pine needles to serve as a foundation for the sleeping bag. Not any more. Try hacking away at a tree on federal or state park land today, and you'll end up in a hassle with a ranger. Also imagine what a pitch-pine stain looks like on a $95 sleeping bag. Finally, these devices are time consuming. You will seldom find exactly what you need where you need it.

Enter the foam pad. Made of urethane, it is light in weight and insulates effectively. While it may not be the perfect solution to the mattress problem, it comes close.

Such pads are available in several different sizes, but unless you're going to be camping on frozen ground or in snow country, the shortie, or hip length pad, is what is recommended. Its size is thirty-six inches by twenty inches by one and one-half inches, it weighs one pound two ounces, and it costs less than $10.

Although the foam pad is bulky, it's a very practical item around the campsite. You can kneel on it while tending the fire. You can lounge around on it. It has a dozen uses and you might want to invest in one despite its bulk.

A foam pad beneath the bag is a must.
(*National Park Service Photo; Fred E. Mang, Jr.*)

Stuff Bags

The way to pack and carry the pad, and the sleeping bag, too, is by making use of a stuff bag, a small cylindrical bag that closes at one end by means of a drawstring. Stuff bags are standard items in camping equipment stores. The best are made of waterproofed nylon and cost no more than $3.

The first step is roll up the foam pad and slide it into the stuff bag. Allow the pad to unroll so there's an opening down the center. Stuff one corner of the sleeping bag down to the very bottom of the opening, and keep stuffing, a handful at a time. Pack the bottom of the opening solidly and the entire bag will go in easily. If it all won't go in, start over again. The final step, of course, is to slide the filled stuff bag into the appropriate compartment of your pack.

The stuff bag will protect the sleeping bag and pad from wear and tear and keep it dry. At night, fill the stuff bag with your daytime clothing. Not only does it serve as a dry place to keep your clothes, but you can use it as your pillow. In fact, some companies refer to it as a pillow sack.

Air Mattresses

There's nothing wrong with an air mattress that a patch kit can't cure. That's the problem; they spring leaks, or, worse, they develop pinholes that are almost impossible to detect, yet in the morning you wake up flat on the ground.

If you're willing to put up with these inconveniences, you will find that the air mattress supports your body in regal fashion. You seem to be floating, which, in actuality, I guess you are.

An air mattress weighs about two pounds. You can buy them in either hip-length or full-length sizes. Specify coated nylon fabric. Rubberized canvas is more durable but it weighs more. Cost: $9 or $10. Don't fail to buy the patch kit, too.

Inspect the ground carefully before you put down the mattress. Remove twigs, sharp stones and pine needles. It is a good idea to use some type of ground cover under the bag to protect against punctures. A sheet of plastic or a poncho will do.

Don't try to inflate the mattress so much that it becomes as hard as a bicycle tire. You'll get the greatest comfort if it is somewhat limp. When you can lie on it and just barely feel your

*Rolled foam pad
is slid in first,
then sleeping bag
is stuffed in.
(Gerry Division;
Outdoor Sports Industries)*

hip bone touch the ground at one point, the mattress is sufficiently inflated.

When you lie on the bag, the valve end should be at your head. Then you are able to make adjustments in the air supply without great effort. When you awaken in the morning, roll over and open the valve and let the air flow out. This will save you the time and effort of doing it later, and lying on the cold, hard ground will give you the incentive you need to get up.

Using the Sleeping Bag

Don't unpack your sleeping bag and crawl right into it. Lay it out and give it time to fluff up. Shake it occasionally.

Don't wear any articles of daytime clothing in the bag unless they are clean and perfectly dry.

One disadvantage of the mummy bag is that it is confining. With a rectangular bag, when you turn your body during the night there's no problem. With a mummy bag, when you turn the bag turns. For some this takes a bit of getting used to.

Care of Sleeping Bags

Air the sleeping bag after use. Simply open it up and spread it out.

When you store the bag at home, hang it in a closet or keep it loosely rolled. Don't store it for long periods in its stuff bag.

After the bag gets twenty-to twenty-five nights of use, it should be cleaned. Wash it yourself, using a bathtub and a mild soap (Woolite is good) — never detergent — and lukewarm water.

Avoid twisting or wringing the fabric. This can tear apart the sewed partitions. Simply work the suds into the fabric by kneading. Rinse and repeat the process several times, and then rinse thoroughly.

Be careful how you take the bag out of the tub. Don't grab it as if it were a suitcase. Get your arms underneath to lift it.

The bag should be tumble-dried, with the drier set for a delicate fabric. *Better Camping* suggests putting a pair of sneakers in with the bag. "The combination of rubber and nylon," says the magazine, "will build up a static electric charge that will allow for full lofting of the down. Also, the weight of the sneakers hitting the bag will tend to break up clumps of wet down that might remain."

The alternative to hand washing is dry cleaning, but you must be especially careful here. Most dry cleaning solvents are simply too harsh for down and remove its natural oils. Colin Fletcher says the solvents used should be petroleum-based, and that usually only the larger cleaning establishments have them.

Tents

"I made my bed in a nook of the pine-thicket," John Muir, camping in the Sierras, noted in his journal, "where the branches were pressed and crinkled overhead like a roof, and bent down around the sides. These are the best bedchambers the high mountains afford — snug as squirrel-nests, well-ventilated, full of spicy odors, and with plenty of wind-layed needles to sing one to sleep."

It's true — tents, under most conditions, are superfluous, although John Muir probably would have had a stronger term.

If you have a good sleeping bag, a mummy bag, you can sleep out almost anywhere in the United States during all of the summer and much of the fall, and never feel really uncomfortable. Tents are for when you expect to encounter extra-cold weather, snow or extended periods of rain. They protect against insects, too. If you should happen to find yourself in the Maine woods during the blackfly season or in Canada's Selkirk Mountains when the mosquitoes are at their fullness, you will want a tent just to eat your lunch in.

There are tents and there are tents. The dictionary says that a tent is "a portable shelter usually of canvas or skins stretched over a supporting framework of poles, ropes and pegs." The words to remember are "a portable shelter." That's all a tent really is. Don't necessarily think in terms of an elaborate, expensive piece of equipment to be purchased from a sporting goods dealer.

A tent can be as basic as a nine-by-twelve-foot sheet of plastic. It can be a big plastic tube. The Rupe family, whose experiences are set down in *Backpacking in the National Forest Wilderness*, carried tubular plastic for shelter, the type of material that garments are wrapped in by dry cleaners, except that it was a bit thicker and of greater circumference. "For it they paid less than seventy-five cents a yard," the booklet declares, "and their tents were about four yards long to accommodate two.

"The plastic weighs little and folds up into a small package. Putting a poncho under for a ground cover is advisable: it is easily puntured."

In using seamless polyethelene tubing as shelter, string a ridge rope between two trees. You don't need pegs, of course. Your sleeping bag will hold the bottom of the cylinder in place. Such tents are well worth carrying and pitching if you're in an area where thunderstorm activity is likely.

A poncho or a groundsheet can also serve as a portable shelter. Again, string a ridge rope between two trees, and weigh down the sides of the poncho with rocks. Heavier ponchos have grommets along the edges and these will enable you to lash the sides to trees or bushes. Of course, you can have grommets installed if you wish.

Bear in mind that this type of shelter is not going to have the traditional tent shape. If your poncho is of average size, the peak height of the structure is not likely to be any more than two feet.

Never lay a poncho or plastic sheet over your bag before going to sleep. Doing this prevents the bag from "breathing" and excessive condensation is likely to result. There has to be plenty of air circulating between the bag and the cover, and that's the reason for the ridge rope.

Buying a Tent

The chief function of the backpacker's tent is to keep the occupants dry in the rain. The tent must also be light in weight and insect-proof, but these are secondary.

The problem that confronts manufacturers is that no light-weight tent can be completely waterproof unless it is made of material which does not let air through. Then the problem of condensation arises.

Try to compress the moisture given off by the human body in the form of exhaled breath and what is called insensible perspiration into a closed-in space, such as a small, plastic-coated tent, and the relative humidity will continue to build until the dew point is reached. The result is a soppy tent, steamy-hot in the summer and damp in the winter.

Even ventilation will not overcome the problem. Wherever moist air comes in contact with the tent's inner surface, condensation will result. It can become so bad that the inner surface of the roof will actually drip water.

Manufacturers solved the condensation problem by developing a two-layer tent. The inner layer is made of light, breathable nylon, while the outer layer, called a rainfly, is plastic-coated nylon. This system enables the tent fabric to attain a temperature

A simple tarp tent.
(*Camp and Trail Outfitters; Camp Trails*)

The rainfly solves the condensation problem. This two man "Backpacker" weighs five pounds, costs less than $40. (Winchester)

higher than the dew point, so that the moist air can pass through without condensing. Of course, the outer layer also serves as protection against the rain, hot sun or whatever.

Besides a rainfly, tents for backpackers come equipped with guy lines, sectional aluminum poles and pegs — and yet weigh no more than four or five pounds. Select a tent the floor of which is made of plastic-coated nylon and that is sewn in all around, preferably above the ground level. Pitched in a well-drained area, a tent with a waterproof, sewn-in floor eliminates the need to dig into the ground cover, a one-time tradition among campers known as ditching the tent.

One rule of thumb states that the tent should be large enough to provide about fourteen square feet of floor space per person, and high enough to allow the occupants to just sit up. Check for mosquito netting and proper ventilation. The door and window should zip tightly shut. It's best if the door and window open from the top down, a feature that allows that warmer air that collects at higher levels to be expelled when they are just barely open.

This two-man backpacking tent weighs 3½ pounds. It is 7¼′ x 4′ and has a peak height of 33 inches.
(*Camp Trails*)

Glacier tents in a Rocky Mountain setting.
(*Sierra Designs*)

The hollow aluminum tent pole should break down into sections of less than three feet. To carry the poles, lash them vertically to your packframe. The tent pegs should be not much larger than your thumb and weigh about one-half ounce each.

Two-man tents with fly covers begin at about $90. One model, mady by Himalayan, weighs only two and a half pounds, but most are about twice that weight. When making inquiries as to weight, be sure that the figure you are given includes the poles and pegs. Also inquire as to the folded-up size of the tent, a statistic that is as important as the floor size.

You can reduce weight and lower cost by buying a single-layer tent, sometimes called a tarp tent, the type that pitches by stringing nylon cord or rope between trees. You can purchase a tarp tent for about $40. One can be carried in a corner of your pack, or, if you want, in your hip pocket. But with tents of this type it is wise to carry two yards of fifty-four-inch plastic which can be stretched as a fly above the tent. This will weigh about four ounces.

In packing your tent, if you know you are going to be in a wooded area where stake material will be available, you can save weight by leaving the stakes and poles behind. Use pieces of wood as pegs and the ridge rope system suggested with the poncho (see above).

Pitching the Tent

Wrinkles and sags will prevent your tent from functioning efficiently. Strive for a tightly-pitched tent.

Begin by lying down on the area you have selected and moving about to be sure that the ground is going to be comfortable. Then stake out the tent floor. Draw the fabric as tight as possible. If there are any diagonal wrinkles in the fabric, the floor is not going to be square.

Next, erect the head with poles and guy lines. The fabric will then drape from the peak to each of the rear corners. Be sure that one side does not sag more than the other. If the drape is not symmetrical, check the guy lines, or perhaps one corner is lower than the other.

Once the head end is up and adjusted properly, erect the other end. Should any sags or wrinkles now appear, it's likely that you will be able to correct them by simply adjusting the angle or tension of a guy line. The final step is to pull out the remaining guy lines, a pair at a time.

Trying to pitch a tent in the wind can be a monstrous experience. Plan to face the front end of the tent into the wind. The first thing to do, even before you unfold the tent, is to drive in the first peg, part way. Then, with the tent still folded, hook the related line over the peg and drive it all the way in. Begin unfolding the tent slowly, weighting down the fabric with rocks.

When the tent is unfolded and weighted down, drive in the rest of the pegs. Then put up the pole and the guy lines. Check the pegs occasionally to see that they don't work loose.

After staking out the tent floor, erect the head poles.
(National Park Service Photo; Fred E. Mang, Jr.)

CHAPTER EIGHT
Where to Camp

A New Yorker who wants to hike can take a West Side subway north to Van Cortlandt Park, a good-sized chunk of rocky, hilled terrain. While not exactly unspoiled, it is at least challenging in spots.

Cook County Forest Preserve is only a thirty-minute drive from downtown Chicago, and there's also the Illinois Prairie Path, the roadbed of the now defunct Chicago, Aurora and Elgin Railroad.

Granted, these locations hardly rival the High Sierra for ruggedness or scenic grandeur, but they make a point. It is almost certain that there is excellent hiking and camping terrain within easy striking distance of where you live. While this chapter focuses on some of the more celebrated backpacker's trails and regions, the place to begin looking is just beyond your backyard.

Inquire about what's available in your city or municipal park systems. Check with local hiking clubs. The Chamber of Commerce is likely to be helpful.

Write to the Department of Conservation and Recreation at

the state capital and request information. The hiking and camping facilities operated by your state may surprise you. For instance, the Adirondack-Champlain area of New York contains some 750,000 acres of state-owned, state-operated land, an area that's three times the size of the much more renowned Mt. Rainier National Park. It's only one of the 120 areas under the jurisdiction of New York State Department of Commerce.

If you're planning on traveling the northeastern part of the country during the summer, consider hiking the ski resorts — the White Mountains area of New Hampshire, the Green Mountains and Sugar Bush Valley in Vermont and the Berkshires of Western Massachusetts. These states, and Maine, offer old farmlands which are ideal for an overnight or a weekend trek.

New England isn't entirely rolling, wooded hills. There's also Cape Cod, where the National Park Service maintains several marked trails.

Palisades Interstate Park, within quick reach of New York City and the heavily populated areas of northern New Jersey, offers thirteen miles of gently winding trails along the Hudson's steep slopes, an excellent prep for the Adirondacks. For additional information, write Palisades Interstate Park (Administration Headquarters, Bear Mountain, New York 10911).

New York City, indeed, mid-Manhattan, boasts a hiking club, which schedules dozens of day-long outings from March through November in areas fifty to one hundred miles from New York City. It's the Chalet Club (135 East 55th St., New York, N.Y. 10022). Write for more information.

New Jersey offers several excellent county parks in Essex, Union, Bergen and Morris Counties, and two thousand acres of land with marked trails on the Watchung Reservation in Union County.

From the Pennsylvania border as far south as Florida, state and federal parks are to be found in abundance, many with trails for backpackers. One of the most renowned is the Chesapeake and Ohio Canal towpath, now under Federal jurisdiction. It stretches along the north bank of the Potomac River from Seneca to Cumberland, Maryland. For more information, write Chesapeake and Ohio Canal National Monument (479 North Potomac St., Hagerstown, Md. 21720).

Washington, D.C. hikers find pleasant trails on Theodore Roosevelt Island in the Potomac. There is a section of the Chesapeake and Ohio Canal towpath beginning in Georgetown.

The Midwest has several types of hiking — rolling farmland, heavily forested hills and lake wilderness areas. Here, as in the south, state parks offer some of the best trails available.

Indiana presents a hiking and camping experience that's different. In Indiana Dunes State Park, located on Lake Michigan in the northwest corner of the state, the trails are laid out between hummocks of wind blown sand. In Wisconsin, there's Kettle Moraine State Forest, strewn with stones and boulders and other debris carried and deposited by the great glaciers. Its trails have been lauded by the Sierra Club's Great Lakes chapter. The trails of Illinois' Beach State Park have been similarly praised.

The Southwest offers state parks, too, but also millions of acres of federally administered parkland. The trails in these areas are well marked and presided over by knowledgeable park rangers, an important fact in this region where the climate tends toward extremes and the terrain can be very difficult.

The Mountain States and the Pacific Coast offer a wealth of federal park land also, but don't overlook state park preserves, or those administered by municipal authorities.

Trail Systems

Much of the backcountry regions of the National Forests, National Parks and state park preserves are crisscrossed by backpacking trails. These vary widely in character, from well-worn, frequently traveled routes, with formal although rudimentary accommodations, to those that amount to barely discernible footpaths. These trails are to be found in every part of the country. The major ones include:

THE APPALACHIAN TRAIL   This is one of the country's best known trails and a favorite among Eastern backpackers. A 1,995-mile footpath, with a chain of lean-tos and fireplaces at eight-mile intervals, the Appalachian trail stretches along America's eastern backbone from Mount Katahdin in Maine to Springer Mountain in Georgia, passing through thirteen states and eight National Forests. It is used for anything from a one-day hike to three-month summertime trek.

Every type of terrain is encountered. In Maine, the trail snakes its way through a wilderness of lakes, streams and mountains. In Massachusetts, the trail ascends Mount Greylock

and winds into the Berkshire Hills before leading on to the scenic valleys of northeastern Connecticut. It crosses the Chesapeake and Ohio Canal towpath in Maryland and passes through historic Harper's Ferry. The wildest parts of the trail are encountered in the Great Smoky Mountains National Park. After dipping sharply out of the Great Smokies to the Little Tennessee River and Fontana Dam, the trail heads east and south into Georgia, then turns back again to its terminus at Springer Mountain.

Throughout much of its length, the trail is easily accessible from major cities and main roads. For information, write the Appalachian Trail Conference (17 N Street, N.W., Washington, D.C. 20036).

THE PACIFIC COAST TRAIL   Hikers and campers in the West backpack the Pacific Coast Trail, which crests towering mountain ridges over much of its 2,156-mile length. It begins at Mount Baker in Washington, then follows the rugged and primitive ridges of the Cascade Mountains, penetrating dense stands of Douglas fir and traversing vast Alpine meadows and long, narrow mountain crests. The scenery is seldom less than spectacular.

Leaving Oregon, the trails coincide with the John Muir Trail in the Sierras and crosses several national parks — Lassen Volcanic National Park, Yosemite, Sequoia and King's Canyon — on its way to the Mojave Desert, the Sierra Madre and San Bernardino Ranges, and the Mexican border, where it ends.

Overall, the Pacific Coast Trail is more rugged than the Appalachian Trail, and lean-to shelters are seldom encountered. The trail is well marked, however. For more information, write: the Pacific Coast Trail System Conference (Hotel Green, 50 Green St., Pasadena, California).

THE FLORIDA TRAIL   This trail provides some of the most unusual vistas in the country — primitive cypress swamps, grassy savannas, broad plains of tropical palms and rolling hillland carpeted with pine forests. It basks in sunshine twelve months a year.

The Florida Trail begins in the southern part of the state, about four miles east of Monroe Station. It winds north into the

Hikers on the Tuckerman Ravine Trail, an access trail to Mount Washington and the Appalachian Trail.
(*U.S. Forest Service*)

dank wilderness of Big Cypress Swamp, intersecting the Everglades Parkway at Mile 39, and then continues north through the swamps and savannas of the Devil's Garden, cross the Caloosahatchie River at Ortona. Along the north shore of Lake Okeechobee, the trail mounts dikes and stretches north to the upper reaches of the St. Johns River at Ortona. It then heads through pine and palmetto, keeping east of Orlando and south of Sanford and plunges into the Ocala National Forest. Gold Head State Park and Osceola National Forest are covered before the trail breaks into the rolling hills south of Tallahassee. Its northern terminus is Panama City on the Gulf of Mexico.

For more information concerning the route, write the Florida Trail Association (33 S.W. 18th Terrace, Miami, Florida 33129).

THE LONG TRAIL New Englanders hike this route, a 255-mile slash through heavily wooded mountains that begins at the Canadian border, bisects Vermont and ends in Western Massachusetts. It is well marked and there are many shelters along the way. For more information, write The Green Mountain Club (108 Merchants Row, Rutland, Vermont 05701).

THE BAKER TRAIL This is convenient for Pennsylvanians. Just over one hundred miles in length, it begins at Freeport on the Allegheny River north of Pittsburgh and extends north to Cook Forest State Park. It is well marked and has shelters every twelve miles. For more information, write Pittsburgh Council, American Youth Hostels (6300 Fifth Ave., Pittsburgh, Pennsylvania 15232).

THE HORSESHOE TRAIL As the name implies, horseback riders use this trail frequently, but it's excellent for backpacking, too. The trail begins just west of Philadelphia at Valley Forge and heads almost due west for 121 miles, meeting the Appalachian Trail at Sharp Mountain, twelve miles north of Hershey. For more information, write Horse-Shoe Trail Club, Inc. (c/o William Nelson West, 1600 Three Center Plaza Philadelphia, Pennsylvania 19102).

THE FINGER LAKES TRAIL When completed, this elaborate trail system through New York state's Finger Lakes region will extend from the Catskill State Park in the south-central part of the state to Bruce Trail in Ontario. Many spur trails

Hikers head out into the Deschutes and Willamette National Forests of Oregon's Cascades.
(U.S.D.A. Forest Service Photo; Jim Hughes)

along the lakes are also being planned. The system is about one-third complete. For more information, write Finger Lakes Trail Association (2783 Brighton-Henrietta Town Line Road, Rochester, New York 14623).

THE BRUCE TRAIL Extending almost five hundred miles along the magnificent Niagara escarpment from Queenston to Tobermory, the Bruce Trail offers sharp contrasts. Some sections are well marked and have shelters, but others traverse dense wilderness and you'll require a good map, a compass and plenty of experience. For more information, write Bruce Trail Association (33 Hardale Crescent, Hamilton, Ontario, Canada).

THE NORTH COUNTRY TRAIL Once this trail has been rehabilitated and, in some areas, rerouted, it can serve for a summer-long trek — at least. It leaves the Appalachian Trail near Lake Champlain in Vermont and crosses New York in westerly direction, paralleling the Pennsylvania border. Then it's into Ohio and north and west to Michigan. From Michigan's Upper Peninsula, the trail heads west across Wisconsin and Minnesota to the Lewis and Clark Trail in North Dakota. Many sections of the North Country Trail are now open.

SHORE-TO-SHORE TRAIL The shores in question are Michigan's. Hold your left hand in front of you, palm down. It's shape is the same as Michigan's lower peninsula. The Shore-to-Shore Trail begins at Elberta on Lake Michigan (relatively, at about the middle joint of your little finger) and crosses the state in a northeasterly direction, ending at Tawas City on Lake Huron (at the middle knuckle of your index finger). It is about two hundred miles long. For more information, write the Michigan Department of Conservation (Lansing, Michigan 48926).

THE BUCKEYE TRAIL One day this trail will extend across southern Ohio and then head north toward Lake Erie. About 150 miles are already completed. For more information, write the Buckeye Trail Association, Box 758, Logan, Ohio 43138.

Apalachicola National Forest, Florida.
(U.S. Forest Service)

Backpacking on Federal Lands

Together the National Parks and National Forests offer some 883,000 square miles for your use and enjoyment, an area the size of two Californias and a Georgia.

While there is no denying that campsites within many federally operated lands are about as private as a Coney Island beach on a summer Sunday, the back country areas of the Parks and Forests present an almost unrivaled opportunity for solitude. It is a matter of fact that a mere 2 percent of the visitors to the National Parks venture beyond the often clogged park roads and established campgrounds to see what lies within.

The National Parks

In the summer of 1870, a party of hardy Montana backpackers explored the awesome wilderness area drained by the Yellowstone River, a region near where the borders of Wyoming, Idaho and Montana come together. The scenic grandeur so inspired them that they vowed the region must be preserved as vast public park. Out of their efforts came Yellowstone National Park, established in 1872 as a "pleasuring ground for the benefit and enjoyment of the people," and, ultimately, the National Park System.

Today there are seventy-eight National Parks in operation and many of them offer vast expanses of back country, areas unreachable by automobile. They range in character from mountain areas of alpine quality to burning deserts. There are seashores and mangrove labyrinths.

The National Park Service is composed of a headquarters staff in Washington (Interior Building, Washington, D.C. 20240), and six regional offices which are as follows.

Northeast Region
143 South 3rd St.
Philadelphia, Penna. 19106

Southwest Region
Box 728
Sante Fe, New Mexico 87501

Southeast Region
Federal Building
Richmond, Va. 23240

Western Region
450 Golden Gate Ave.
San Francisco, Calif. 94102

Midwest Region
1709 Jackson St.
Omaha, Neb. 68102

Northwest Region
Fourth and Pike Building
Seattle, Wash. 98101

Within the jurisdiction of these regional offices are the seventy-eight national parks, monuments, buildings, recreation areas and historic sites. But it is the areas that offer backcountry hiking and camping that should interest you the most. The pages that follow list and briefly describe the best of these. For more information on any one, write the park superintendent.

You should be aware that you are subject to a number of rules and regulations when traveling Park Service backcountry. Camping permits are required and so are fire permits. No vehicles, including trail bikes, are permitted, nor is hunting allowed.

Gathering of firewood, where allowed, is restricted to dead wood *on the ground*. You cannot pick wild flowers or collect rock specimens. You are urged to inform a park ranger of your plans if your hike is going to be overnight or any longer.

All combustible refuse has to be burned. Anything that's non-combustible has to be carried out.

"Don't smoke while traveling in the forest," say officials. "If you must smoke, stop, finish your cigarette, and cover it with soil before going on."

The following are the parks.

BADLANDS NATIONAL MONUMENT (Box 72, Interior, S.D. 57750) This aptly-named chunk of eroded landscape consists largely of sharp ridges and steep-walled canyons. Fossils of prehistoric mammals are to be found in the sedimentary deposits. The inhabitants nowadays are coyotes, badgers, jackrabbits, deer, prairie dogs and golden eagles. Expect temperature extremes and sudden storms. Trails, aside from packhorse routes, are limited in number. Not for the novice.

BIG BEND NATIONAL PARK (Big Bend National Park, Texas 79834) This is Rio Grande country — mountain ranges and sharp-walled canyons plus vast desert expanses. The park is abundant in fossil remains. Its present day population includes cougar, coyote, pronghorn, pecary, coati, deer and bobcat, not to mention lizards and snakes. Horses are allowed on 162 of the park's 174 miles of trails.

BIGHORN CANYON NATIONAL RECREATION AREA (Box 458, Hardin, Montana 59035) No trails here but backpackers are welcome. All you need is a fire permit or, if you plan to camp on the Crow Reservation, which is included in the area, you'll require a tribal permit. Although this is classified as an arid region by the park service, it is bisected by a seventy-one-mile long reservoir, the lower two-thirds of which lie within rugged, steep-walled canyons, where fossil remains can be found. Elk, deer, beaver, black bear and wild horses populate the area.

CANYONLANDS NATIONAL PARK (First Western Building, 72 South Main St., Moab, Utah 84532) At the junction of the Green and Colorado Rivers in east central Utah, this park, with its canyons and wind eroded sandstone formations, is a geological wonderland. Part of it is desert country, scattered with green oases, but there are also mountains as high as 7,800 feet. Summer and autumn are best for hiking. Bring plenty of water.

CHANNEL ISLANDS NATIONAL MONUMENT (P.O. Box 1388, Oxnard, Calif. 93030) For a really unusual hiking experience, take a boat at Oxnard and head south to Anacapa or Santa Barbara Island, a fifty-mile trip. There are sandy beaches, cragged headlands, quiet coves and rookeries of sea mammals and birds. There are no established trails but sites for camping have been provided. You have to pack along drinking water.

CRATER LAKE NATIONAL PARK (P.O. Box 7, Crater Lake, Oregon) Crystal-clear Crater Lake in the heart of a dead volcano, its lava walls as high as half a mile, is the chief attraction here. The park is traversed by the Pacific Crest Trail (see above).

CRATERS OF THE MOON NATIONAL MONUMENT (P.O. Box 29, Arco, Idaho) Vast lava fields pocked with huge cinder-walled depressions give this area a genuine lunar look. Though austere, even desolate, it supports many species of plant and animal life. There are no campsites and no trails, but the park service allows you to strike out on your own.

Angel Arch is one of the sights at Canyonlands National Park. (Utah Tourist & Publicity Council; Ward Roylance)

Craters of the Moon National Monument.
(National Park Service)

CUMBERLAND GAP NATIONAL HISTORICAL PARK (P.O. Box 840, Middlesboro, Kentucky) The forested mountain pass of Daniel Boone's Wilderness Road, the main artery of the great trans-Allegheny migration, is memorialized by this park. There are forty-two miles of trails, and on thirty-four of them horses are permitted. Hiking guides are available.

DEATH VALLEY NATIONAL MONUMENT (Death Valley, Calif. 92328) While this park presents the lowest-lying land in the Western Hemisphere — 282 feet below sea level — it also offers mountains that range to eleven thousand feet. Only eight miles of trails, but cross-country hiking is permitted. "Not for summer hiking," advises the park service.

DINOSAUR NATIONAL MONUMENT (P.O. Box 101, Dinosaur, Colorado 81610) Tucked into the northwest corner of Colorado at the confluence of the turbulent Green and Yampa Rivers, this park offers some of the world's most striking dinosaur-fossil deposits. The scenic views are spectacular, too, especially the sheer river canyons. There are eight miles of foot trails, thirty miles of jeep trails, and you also have the option of trekking cross-country, but check with a park ranger first.

EVERGLADES NATIONAL PARK (P.O. Box 279, Homestead, Florida 33030) Billed as the largest subtropical wilderness in the United States, this 1½-million-acre park offers 44 miles of foot trails and 120 miles of canoe trails. Much of this river of grass teems with wildlife — bobcat, cougar, whitetail deer, crocodiles and an infinite variety of wading birds. Plan to bring drinking water. A detailed waterway guide is available for $2.50.

GLACIER BAY NATIONAL MONUMENT (Gustavus, Alaska 99826) An unrivaled show; great geologic forces tear mountainous blocks of ice loose from the mainland and plunge them into the sea, creating thundering waves and massive icebergs. There's no access by land; only by airplane from nearby Juneau.

GLACIER NATIONAL PARK (West Glacier, Montana 59936) Perched on the Rocky Mountains closeby the U.S.-Canadian border, this park, with its glaciers, knife-edged ridges, forests, lakes and alpine glades, has long been a favorite among Western backpackers. It offers nine hundred miles of foot trails, and backcountry camping, except for a fire permit, is unrestricted.

GLEN CANYON NATIONAL RECREATION AREA (P.O. Box 1507, Page, Arizona 86040)   Long fingers of Lake Powell, formed by waters backed against the massive Glen Canyon Dam, provide access to the farthest reaches of this park's countless canyons astride tributaries of the Colorado River. The dam is one of the world's engineering marvels. The fishing is good but you must bring drinking water.

GRAND CANYON NATIONAL PARK (P.O. Box 129, Grand Canyon, Arizona 86023)   One of the most celebrated backpacking areas in the country, Grand Canyon National Park and National Monument offer 239 miles of trails, countless cross-country hiking opportunities and float trips on the Colorado River. You choose either the canyon's South or North Rim. The South Rim, at 7,000 feet, is a flat, pine-forested plateau. The North Rim, less developed and less traveled, is around 1,800 feet higher, and thus cooler and not so dry. If you're a beginner, the South Rim is recommended.

GRAND TETON NATIONAL PARK (P.O. Box 67, Moose, Wyoming 83012)   Lofty, glacier-carved peaks, their slopes forested with conifers and aspens, and a multitude of large and small lakes are the reasons this park has become a mecca for hikers and mountain climbers. There are 175 miles of trails, and the fishing is good.

GREAT SMOKY MOUNTAINS NATIONAL PARK (Gatlinburg, Tennessee 37738)   An extensive trail system, more than six hundred miles in length with twenty-one shelters, makes the Great Smokies a hiker's paradise. The area, which offers the loftiest peaks east of the Mississippi, is extraordinarily rich in plantlife, including some 1,400 kinds of flowering plants, some of the biggest broadleaf trees in the United States and great forests of conifers. A free hiking guide and a brochure on winter camping are available.

An overlook at Dinosaur National Monument.
(National Park Service)

HALEAKALA NATIONAL PARK (P.O. Box 456, Kahului, Maui, Hawaii 96732) A dormant volcanic crater, one of the largest and most colorful in the world, make this a unique hiking experience. There are thirty-five miles of trails with camping permitted only at established sites. Conditions are best suited for a two- or three-day trek. Be prepared for hot sun but also bring rainwear.

HAWAII VOLCANOES NATIONAL PARK (Hawaii Volcanoes National Park, Hawaii 96718) Like Haleakala National Park, this park includes volcanic terrain, but the volcanoes here are active. It also offers lush lowlands and ocean shore. There are 133 miles of trails and four shelters. Note that the park is located on the island of Hawaii. Access is by air from Honolulu.

ISLE ROYALE NATIONAL PARK (87 North Ripley St., Houghton, Minn. 49931) If you're planning on backpacking through the upper midwest, be sure to consider Isle Royale, a one-hundred-mile strip of land in Lake Superior off Minnesota's northeast corner. It's large enough to support more than thirty of its own lakes, some of them with islands of their own. In sum, it is a lake-and-wood wilderness, one of the most primitive regions in the United States. There are no roads and only four shelters for the park's 160 miles of trails. Access to the park is by park-service boat from Houghton, or a charter boat from Copper Harbor, Michigan.

JOSHUA TREE NATIONAL MONUMENT (P.O. Box 875, Twentynine Palms, Calif. 92277) Joshua tree is a type of yucca, with great sword-shaped leaves and greenish-white flowers. In this desert plateau land, the tree attains a height of forty-feet. There are also spidery ocotillo, colorful cactuses and other desert flora along the fifty miles of trails.

KATMAI NATIONAL MONUMENT (P.O. Box 7, King Salmon, Alaska 99613) This volcanic region of the Aleutian Range, located about 250 miles south of Anchorage, is, at 2,792,000 acres, the largest area in the National Park System. Part forest, part grassland, part tundra, it is interlaced with streams and studded with lakes. It is reachable only by airplane.

St. Mary's Lake, Glacier National Park.
(National Park Service)

LAKE MEAD NATIONAL RECREATION AREA (601 **Nevada Highway, Boulder City, Nevada 89005**) This is desert country but despite the bright sun and high summer temperatures, low humidity makes for comfort and the nights are cool. And it's not all desert. The park includes lofty plateaus, deep canyons and all the recreational opportunities a lake area implies. There are no formal trails but cross-country foot and horse travel are practically unlimited.

LASSEN VOLCANIC NATIONAL PARK (Mineral, Calif. 96063) Lassen Peak, a symmetrical cinder cone volcano that reaches 10,452 feet, with fumaroles, hot springs and lava beds, is the chief feature here — but it's not the only one. There are other mountains, wilderness lakes and coniferous forests. Cross-country travel is "not advisable," says the park system. "Camp only at established sites along trails."

LAVA BEDS NATIONAL MONUMENT (P.O. 867, Tulelake, Calif. 96134) Although spring flower beds bloom wherever there is sufficient soil, the landscape here is largely barren and grim, and dotted with cinder cones and craters. Horses are allowed on the forty-four miles of trails.

MOUNT McKINLEY NATIONAL PARK (P.O. Box 9, McKinley Park, Alaska) This is almost two million acres of Alaskan wilderness — alpine tundra, spruce forests, glacial streams and lakes, and the loftiest mountain peak in North America. For wildlife there's caribou, moose, black and grizzly bear, wolverine, lynx, river otter — the list goes on and on. Anchorage, about 150 miles to the south, is the embarkation point for park travel.

MOUNT RAINIER NATIONAL PARK (Longmire, Wash. 98397) Towering Mount Rainier, 14,408 feet high, a dormant ice-clad volcanic peak, not only dominates this park but much of the entire state. Its craterlike summit is a challenge to mountain climbers, while its lush dense forest and flower-carpeted alpine meadows at lower altitude are major attractions for hikers. There are 290 miles of trails and thirteen shelters. In backcountry camping is permitted only at established sites.

An aerial view of a portion of Isle Royale National Park. *(National Park Service)*

NORTH CASCADES NATIONAL PARK (Sedro Woolley, Wash. 98284)   Part of a vast recreational complex in the northwest corner of the state, which includes Lake Chelan and Ross Lake National Recreation Areas, this park provides unlimited opportunities for backpacking experiences. Its 159 miles of trails traverse alpine wilderness, deep glaciated canyons, jagged peaks and heavily forested valleys, and presenting vistas of alpine lakes and active glaciers.

OLYMPIC NATIONAL PARK (600 East Park Ave., Port Angeles, Wash. 98362)   There are no interior or trans-park roads here. Anyone who wants to view the two-mile long glaciers, the lush mountain meadows or the rock-bound primitive coastline has to go in on foot. There are six hundred miles of trails; horses are permitted. There is both salt-water and fresh-water fishing.

ORGAN-PIPE CACTUS NATIONAL MONUMENT (P.O. Box 38, Ajo, Ariz. 85321)   Bordering Mexico, about 140 miles south of Phoenix, this is a beautiful land of stark mountains, rocky canyons and arid washes. It is the only area in the United States where tall stands of organ-pipe cactus flourish. Summer hiking can be brutal, with torrid temperatures and violent thunderstorms. Mid-autumn through early spring is the best.

POINT REYES NATIONAL SEASHORE (Point Reyes, Calif. 94956)   A peninsula that juts into the Pacific Ocean off the California coast north of San Francisco, this park presents a varied environment, ranging from sandy beaches and flat grasslands to thick forests and towering rock cliffs. The wildlife is varied, too, from cougar and mule deer to pelicans and sea otter. There are 175 miles of trails and one hundred miles of unsurfaced roads.

REDWOOD NATIONAL PARK (Drawer N, Crescent City, Calif. 95531)   Once a magnificent redwood forest extended hundreds of miles along the Pacific Coast. This park contains the remnants. Besides the redwoods that managed to escape the loggers' saws, there are beaches, dunes, salt marshes and scrubland. There are seventeen miles of trails. Cross-country hiking is not encouraged.

ROCKY MOUNTAIN NATIONAL PARK (Estes Park, Colo. 80517) This is a high-country park with every feature that designation implies — rugged snow-capped peaks, alpine lakes, glacier-sculptured valleys and upland forests. Wildlife abounds. There are thirty-three miles of trails and cross-country travel is permitted in some areas.

SAGUARO NATIONAL MONUMENT (P.O. Box 17210, Tucson, Ariz. 85710) Remarkable giant cactus are a main feature of this desert sanctuary but there is a wide variety of other flora. For example, pine and Douglas fir cover the slopes of both Rincon and Tucson Mountains, which are located within the area. There are sixty-six miles of trails in the park's Rincon Section, twelve in the Tucson section, and cross-country travel is permitted in both.

SEQUOIA NATIONAL PARK; KINGS CANYON NATIONAL PARK (Three Rivers, Calif. 93271) These two adjacent parks offer High Sierra wilderness, with deep canyons, spectacular waterfalls and magnificent forests, which, says the park service, contain groves of the "world's largest living things." There are 775 miles of trails, 715 of which are open to horses, three shelters for summer hikers, one for winter use. Both parks are traversed by the Pacific Crest Trail.

SHENANDOAH NATIONAL PARK (Luray, Virginia 22835) One of the few backcountry areas of the National Park System readily available to Northeastern hikers, this park consists of an eighty-mile-long stretch of the Blue Ridge Mountains and provides magnificent panoramic views of forested mountains and valleys. There are 470 miles of trails. Camping is permitted only at designated sites. There are twenty-one open shelters and five cabins. Write for free maps and a guidebook.

THEODORE ROOSEVELT NATIONAL MEMORIAL PARK (Medora, North Dakota 58645) This area is more for the rider than the hiker, for the landscape of gullies and gorges, hills and ridges, and only occasional patches of prairie, make it rough going on foot.

WHISKEYTOWN RECREATION AREA (P.O. Box 188, Whiskeytown, Calif. 96095) The verdant hills and mountains

surrounding a three-thousand-acre lake are what attract hikers to this area. Camping is unrestricted. There are fifty-seven miles of trails.

YELLOWSTONE NATIONAL PARK (Yellowstone National Park, Wyoming 82190) Everyone knows about Yellowstone, the world's greatest geyser area and notable also for its spectacular waterfalls, canyons and mountain ranges that teem with wildlife. There are eleven hundred miles of trails at Yellowstone, and camping is unrestricted.

YOSEMITE NATIONAL PARK (P.O. Box 577, Yosemite National Park, Calif. 95389) This geological wonderland of the High Sierras, with its sculptered peaks and granite domes, vast forests of conifers and groves of giant sequoias, offers trails for hikes of just a few hours or treks of a week or longer. There are 749 miles of trails in all. Camping is permitted only at established sites.

ZION NATIONAL PARK (Springdale, Utah 84767) This is mesa country, with colorful canyons and wind and water-eroded sandstone the main features. More than 150 miles of trails are available.

National Forests

Within a one-day automobile trip of any point in the United States (excepting Hawaii and Alaska's deep interior), there lies a National Forest. There are 154 in total, plus eighteen national grasslands, and they cover an area of 181 million acres, or about one acre for every United States citizen.

Camping privacy is almost always the keynote in the national forests. Even where planned campsites are to be found, they are at least one hundred feet apart, with plenty of trees and shrubs in between. But the wilderness lands of the National Forests are what are important to the backpacker. Found mostly in high mountain country, these wilderness lands comprise about one-quarter of the National Forest System.

Saguaro cactus at Saguaro National Monument.
(*National Park Service*)

Be prepared to rough it when you enter one of these. There are no roads; no motorized travel of any type is permitted. You have to hike in, ride horseback or paddle a canoe. Even trails, except as noted below, are few.

The program of the U.S. Forest Service to manage and maintain wilderness lands *as wilderness*, as protecting their unspoiled character, began about fifty years ago, in 1924, when a large section of what is now the Gila Wilderness Region of New Mexico was set aside as a specially protected area. Two years later, the Boundary Waters Canoe area in Minnesota was given similar wilderness designation, and in the years that followed the other areas were added.

A significant step forward took place on September 3, 1964, when President Johnson signed into law a bill which created the National Wilderness Preservation System, which directed that fifty-four National Forest Areas were "to remain forever natural," except for certain restricted commercial uses. Another thirty-four areas (5½ million acres) were designated Primitive Area, which meant that they were to be later reviewed for addition to the Wilderness System.

Sweeping east from the Rocky Mountains, lie great rolling plains. These are comprised of the National Grasslands, areas of the country that once suffered terrible abuse, but are now being restored to their original grass cover. Insterspersed with the grasslands are native meadows and fields of wheat and other grains.

Most of these preserves are to be found in the Great Plains States — North and South Dakota, Wyoming, Colorado and Texas. In total, the National Grasslands comprise four million acres.

Hiking and camping are only two of the reasons people are attracted to the National Forest lands. They offer the hunter an unrivaled list of game and they also contain some of the best fishing waters in the world. Among the game animals are moose, antelope, elk, mountain sheep, mountain goats, whitetail and blacktail deer, and black, grizzly and Alaska brown bears. The game birds include wild turkeys and many species of grouse, geese and duck.

So you may want to pack along a rifle or a shotgun. Firearms are allowable in the national forests but they must be used in keeping with state hunting ordinances. Check not only with local state authorities but the forest ranger, too. In most regions, there is something you can hunt all year-round.

Regions of the National Forest Service.

For anyone interested in photography, the national forests abound in subjects. These include seldom seen canyons, gorges and waterfalls; hidden mountain lakes and glaciers, and seemingly infinite stretches of timberland.

This suggests the diverse character of the National Forest wilderness areas. In Alaska's great Tongass National Forest, you can view one of the largest glaciers in the world — Mendenhall Glacier, a glittering two-mile wide and, and in some places a towering two hundred feet high. Or try Ocala National Forest in Florida, where you can swim in crystal clear Alexander Springs, paddle down streams bordered by thick jungle flora and listen to eerie bird calls.

Hikers from the heavily populated areas of the Northeast are within easy reach of the Great Gulf Wilderness area, part of the White Forest National Forest in New Hampshire. The Great Gulf itself, gouged out of the mountains by glaciers, rises from valley depths of 1,600 feet to merge with the eastern slopes of Mount Washington and the Presidential Range, where peaks attain 5,800 feet. Those who have visited the area speak of the deep sense of solitude it creates.

Pisgah National Forest in North Carolina, with two wilderness areas, one at Linville Gorge, the other at Shining Rock, is within striking range of most Eastern hikers. Linville Gorge

Headwaters of the Savannah River in the Pisgah National Forest.
(National Forest Service)

encloses the Linville River and offers steep slopes, overhanging cliffs and unusual rock formations. Shining Rock gets its name from the sharp outcroppings of white quartz that dot the rolling hill land.

For backpackers of the Lake States who enjoy canoe camping, there's no better place than the Boundary Waters Canoe Area of Minnesota, the only lakeland wilderness area under the jurisdiction of the Park System. No one knows for sure how many lakes are here, but there are more than a thousand that are ten acres in size or larger. There are streams and rivers, too. At almost one million acres, this is the largest wilderness area east of the Rocky Mountains.

The southwestern United States offers sharp contrasts in hiking experiences. There are arid desert areas, where there is little besides giant saguaro cactus, tumbleweed, sage and an occasional gila monster. But there are also snow-capped mountains and sheer canyons, some of which once housed cliff-dwelling Indians. Much of it is forbidding territory.

Mazatzal Wilderness Area in the Tonto National Forest, known locally as the Ma-ta-zel wilderness, is, at 205,137 acres, the largest wilderness area in Arizona. Located in the almost precise geographical center of the state, it is recommended to any hiker seeking dramatic scenery and varied wildlife. Elevations range to 7,800 feet, with many peaks carved out of solid rock and separated from one another by narrow, vertical-walled canyons.

The Superstition Wilderness, also in the Tonto National Forest, is rugged, too, but it is largely desert country. The name *Superstition* is derived from the legends surrounding the Lost Dutchman Gold Mine. Many people are said to have died under peculiar circumstances while searching for the mine and its treasure.

New Mexico's Gila Wilderness in the Gila National Forest, the first parcel of public land to win wilderness designation, is part of the state's Mongallan Plateau, an area split by steep canyons and rushing rivers. Besides the spectacular scenery, there's hunting and fishing. The Gila Primitive Area offers unusual geographical, topographical and ecological features. It is rich in history, too — having once been known as Apacheria, or land of the Apache Indians.

Scenic views that are wholly unique for the Southwest are to be found in the San Pedro Parks Wilderness Area, a portion of the Santa Fe National Forest. Here a high, moist plateau of rolling mountains alternates with dense stands of spruce and alpine meadows. It's hard to believe you're in New Mexico. Deer, bear, turkey and grouse attract hunters and, says the Forest Service, "fishermen rarely leave the streams empty-handed."

Most hikers agree that the wilderness areas of the Rocky Mountain Region are the most magnificent of all. This is an area of towering snow-capped mountains with forest-carpeted slopes, steep canyons and sparkling streams. It is difficult to convey its immensity and diversity.

As an example, take La Garita Wilderness Area in Colorado's Gunnison and Rio Grande National Forest. Taking its name from the Spanish words for "the overlook," La Garita features San Luis and Stewart Peaks, both over 14,000 feet, strewn with glacial rock deposits and alive with white water streams containing cutthroat and brook trout.

The largest of the Forest Service's Wilderness tracts, at just under one million acres, is Idaho's Selway-Bitterroot Area in the Bitterroot, Clearwater and Nezperce National Forest. Astride the Bitterroot Range, which forms the boundary between Idaho and Montana, the area is so immense that a year of exploration would leave much of it not only unwalked but unseen. Trails enter the backcountry from all sides. One feature is the huge elk herd, one of the largest in the world, that roams the region.

One of the smallest but more interesting of this region's Wilderness Areas is the Gales of the Mountain Wilderness Area in the Helena National Forest. Named for the mountains that threatened to bar the forward progress of the Lewis and Clark Expedition up the Missouri River, the area offers trails that pass through narrow gorges such as Refrigerator Canyon, named for the cooling winds that never stop blowing. A mosslike phlox covers the rock formations with a brilliant green mantle. Water is scarce because streams sink into fissures and disappear.

Wyoming's North and South Absoroka Wilderness Areas, both part of the Shoshone National Forests, are renowned for their fishing and big-game hunting. There are herds of mountain lion, elk, deer, moose, and bears, including the grizzly. Many of the trails here were first hiked or ridden by the Shoshone Indians, who prized the region for its abundant game.

Wyoming's Teton Wilderness is of special interest because of Two Ocean Pass. Here Two Ocean Creek divides, sending one stream west to the Pacific Ocean, the other to the Atlantic. The area serves as the summer range for the Jackson Hole elk herd.

Crossing a snowfield in the Wallowa-Whitman National Forest of Northeast Oregon.
(U.S.D.A. Forest Service; Jim Hughes)

The wilderness areas of Southern California offer vast desert panoramas framed by rugged, sparsely vegetated mountains. Desert flowers bloom in a riot of color each spring.

Much of the rest of the state is rough and has rugged mountains. The eastern slopes of the Sierra, among the most precipitous in the world, plunge into lush valleys where swift trout streams flow.

Mokelumne Wilderness area in Eldorado and Stanislaus National Forest offers terrain of this type. The area is dominated by barren Mokelumne Peak, which reaches ten thousand feet, and is bisected by the rushing Mokelumne River, which has formed a deep, steep-walled canyon. Within the shallow valleys to the north of Mokelumne Peak, the hiker comes upon small, secluded lakes, the shores of which provide some of the most scenic camping spots in the country. There's wildlife everywhere, including an occasional black bear.

The John Muir Wilderness Area, part of the Inyo and Sierra National Forest, named for the noted naturalist, is the largest Wilderness Area in California and considered to be one of the most inviting in America. Extending along the crest of the Sierra from Mammoth Lakes southward to the slopes of Mount Whitney, it is dominated by snow-capped mountains, their gentle slopes packed with quiet lakes. The region's countless streams are stocked with rainbow, golden and eastern brook trout. Lodgepole pine, red fir and scattered alpine species cover the slopes at lower altitudes.

The Forest Service calls California Ventana Wilderness in Los Padres National Forest "a hiker's paradise." You don't need mountaineering experience because the highest elevation, the summit of Ventana Peak, is "only" 4,833 feet. Birdlife is abundant amidst the stands of ponderosa and Jeffrey pine, native oak and madrona. The rare and beautiful bristle conifer, sometimes called Santa Lucia fir, is also native to the area. But it is the many all-year streams that hold the greatest attraction, for almost all are stocked with rainbow trout. Wild boar, wild pigeon and quail can be hunted in season.

Some California Wilderness Areas are limited to winter use because of the extreme fire hazard that prevails during the summer and fall. The Agua Tibia Primitive Area in the Cleveland National Forest is one such area. What can the winter hiker expect to see? The flora includes desert plants, a great belt of chapparal, mazanita, a type of evergreen shrub which here attains a height of sixteen feet, plus stands of cedar, white fir, big cone Douglas fir and Jeffrey pine. Deer and small-game animals abound, and mountain lions, bobcats and coyotes also populate the area.

Geologists say that the mountain areas of the Pacific Northwest were formed during the Pliocene and early Pleistocene periods, when the entire land mass that is now the Cascade Range was the scene of awesome volcanic activity. Later this area, which extends from the California border across all of Oregon and Washington, was sculpted to its present form by the moving ice of great glaciers.

Hikers and campers visiting the National Forests of these states see the results — volcanic peaks, their uppermost slopes devoid of timber and most other vegetation, and dikes and sills and other such geological formations.

The trees are tall and majestic. Douglas fir and Sitka spruce reach heights exceeding 250 feet, and there are great stands of cedar, white fir and hemlock. Pine forests blanket literally millions of acres, often growing so densely that passage through is difficult. There are a multitude of swift-running mountain streams which originate in the high mountain snow fields.

Oregon's Mt. Hood Wilderness Area offers Mt. Hood itself, believed to be the most frequently climbed snow-covered mountain next to Fujiyama. With guides and proper equipment, novice hikers can attain its summit, which reaches 11,245 feet, without great difficulty. This is in the summer, of course. Only an experienced climber would make the attempt in the winter. The trails on the slopes of Mt. Hood open to foot travel around July 15th, and they are not completely free of snow until mid-August.

The Kalmiopsis Wilderness Area in the Siskiyou National Forest boasts one of the most botanically interesting areas in the Pacific Northwest. A dozen different species of conifers, nine of hardwoods and thirty-one species of shrubs can be found within its borders. The land is rocky and brush-strewn, presenting unusual vistas for this area. There are hazards, however. Rattlesnakes, for instance. And watch out for poison oak.

Washington's Pasaytan Wilderness Area in the Okanogan National Forest presents every imaginable wilderness experience. Located in the extreme northwestern corner of the state, the park is a huge one — twenty miles wide and forty miles in length. Every kind of topography and plant cover native to the Northern Cascades can be found here, and trails vary in degree of difficulty from guided horseback tours to challenging mountain

*View of Greywolf Peak, Flathead National Forest, Montana.
(U.S.D.A. Forest Service; Thad Lowary)*

climbs. The almost one hundred mountain lakes and the Pasayten Rivers and its tributaries are well stocked with fish, chiefly trout of several species. Deer, goat and bear can be hunted in season.

The U. S. Forest System is divided into ten regions, and each with a good number of forests and trails under its jurisdiction. By writing to the Regional Forester at any of the below listed regional headquarters, you can obtain information regarding specific routes, roadway accesses, condition of trails, type of terrain, etc. The list includes all wilderness (W) and primitive (P) areas.

Northern Region
Federal Building
Missoula, Montana 59801

Absaroka, Montana (P)
Anaconda-Pinlar, Montana (W)
Beartooth, Montana (P)
Bob Marshall, Montana (W)
Cabinet Mountains, Montana (W)
Gates of the Mountains, Montana (W)
Mission Mountains, Montana (P)
Salmon River Breaks, Idaho (P)
Selway-Bitterroot, Idaho (W)
Spanish Peaks, Montana (P)

Rocky Mountain Region
Federal Center, Building 85
Denver, Colorado 80225

Cloud Peak, Wyoming (P)
Flat Tops, Colorado (P)
Glacier, Wyoming (P)
Gore Range-Eagle Nest, Colo. (P)
La Garita, Colorado (W)
Maroon Bells-Snowmass, Colo. (W)
Mt. Zirkel, Colorado (W)
North Absaroka, Wyoming (W)
Popo Agie, Wyoming (P)
Rahwah, Colorado (W)
San Juan, Colorado (P)
South Absaroka, Wyoming (W)

Stratified, Wyoming (P)
Upper Rio Grande, Colorado (P)
Uncompahgre, Colorado (P)
West Elk, Colorado (W)
Wilson Mountains, Colorado (P)

Southwestern Region
Federal Building
Albuquerque, New Mexico 87101

Black Range, New Mexico (P)
Blue Range, Arizona (P)
Chiricahua, Arizona (W)
Galiuro, Arizona (W)
Gila, New Mexico (W & P)
Mazatzal, Arizona (W)
Mount Baldy, Arizona (P)
Pecos, New Mexico (W)
Pine Mountain, Arizona (P)
San Pedro Parks, New Mexico (W)
Sierra Ancha, Arizona (W)
Superstition, Arizona (W)
Sycamore Canyon, Arizona (P)
Wheeler Mountain, New Mexico (W)
White Mountain, New Mexico (W)

Intermountain Region
Forest Service Building
Ogden, Utah 84403

Bridger, Wyoming (W)
High Uintas, Utah (P)
Hoover, Colorado & Nevada (W)
Idaho, Idaho (P)
Jarbidge, Nevara (W)
Sawtooth, Idaho (P)
Teton, Wyoming (W)

California Region
630 Sansome Street
San Francisco, California 94111

Agua Tibia, California (P)

Caribou, California (W)
Desolation Valley, California (P)
Devil Canyon-Bear Canyon, California (P)
Dome Lant, California (W)
Emigrant Basin, California (P)
High Sierra, California (P)
Hoover, California & Nevada (W)
John Muir, California (W)
Marble Mountain, California (W)
Minarets, California (W)
Mokelumne, California (W)
San Gorgonio, California (W)
San Jacinto, California (W)
San Rafael, California (P)
South Warner, California (W)
Thousand Lakes, California (W)
Ventana, California (P)
Yolla Bolly-Middle Eel, California (W)

Pacific Northwest Region
Post Office Box 3623
Portland, Oregon 96208

Diamond Peak, Oregon (W)
Eagle Cap, Oregon (W)
Gearhart Mountain, Oregon (W)
Glacier Peak, Washington (W)
Goat Rocks, Washington (W)
Kalmiopsis, Oregon (W)
Mount Adams, Washington (W)
Mount Hood, Oregon (W)
Mount Jefferson, Oregon (P)
Mount Washington, Oregon (W)
Mountain Lakes, Oregon (W)
North Cascades, Washington (P)
Strawberry Mountain, Oregon (W)
Three Sisters, Oregon (W)

Southern Region
50 Seventh Street N.E.
Atlanta, Georgia 30323

Linville Gorge, North Carolina (W)

The Backpacker's Handbook

North Central Region
710 N. 6th Street
Milwaukee, Wisconsin 53203

Boundary Water Canoe Area, Minnesota (P)

Eastern Region
6816 Market Street
Upper Darby, Pennsylvania 19082

Great Gulf, New Hampshire (W)

Alaska Region
Federal Office Building
Juneau, Alaska 99801

Chugach National Forest, Anchorage
North Tongass National Forest, Juneau
South Tongass National Forest, Ketchikan

Puerto Rico

Caribbean National Forest, Rio Piedras

Other Areas

Several other federal agencies adminster areas where hiking and camping are permitted. The Army's Corps of Engineers (Department of the Army, The Pentagon, Washington, D.C. 20310) maintains reservoir areas in forty-one states where camping is possible. The same is true for about one-half of the 140 reservoir areas under the jurisdiction of the U.S. Department of the Interior's Bureau of Reclamation (Washington, D.C. 20240).

Primitive-type camping is also possible on Indian lands under the jurisdiction of the Bureau of Indian Affairs (U.S. Department of the Interior, 1951 Constitution Ave., N.W., Washington, D.C. 20242). However, Indian reservations are private property, and you must obtain permission from the superintendent of the reservation to hike and camp.

Last, there is the Bureau of Sport Fisheries and Wildlife, another arm of the Department of the Interior (Washington,

D.C. 20240). One of the Bureau's objectives is to "operate a nationwide system of wildlife refuges," and many of these are open to hikers and campers.

Canada

Canada is the second largest country in the world, and as this implies it offers an enormous amount of hiking and camping opportunities.

Just trace the route of the Trans-Canada Highway, the longest highway in the world, to get an idea of what the country can present. It begins in the east at St. John's, and as it crosses Newfoundland it touches countless bays, harbors and quaint villages. A ferry provides the link between Newfoundland and Nova Scotia, and then the highway extends across the maritime province of New Brunswick. Attracting hikers to this region is Fundy National Park, which borders the Bay of Fundy, notable for its tides which are among the highest in the world.

Quebec is just to the west, and the country turns French. Mt. Temblant Park is one of the chief attractions of this region. After crossing Ontario, the highway heads across the broad plains of Manitoba. Riding Mountain National Park, in the heart of Manitoba's prairieland, offers hikers thick green woodlands and countless lakes. Winnipeg is the jumping off point for the park.

After the prairies of Saskatchewan and the cattle country of Alberta, the Canadian Rockies begin. Wood National Park, across the northern border of Alberta and extending into Canada's Northwest Territory, is a vast preserve where the flat prairieland meets dense forests.

Better known and more frequently trekked is the mountain wilderness of Jasper National Park on the Alberta-British-Columbia border and, just south of it, Banff National Park, which offers some of the world's most thrilling scenery.

British Columbia, bordered on the west by the Pacific, on the north by the sub-Arctic, and on the east by the Rockies, presents hiking to suit every taste. There are four National Parks in British Columbia. Water Lakes National Park, which abuts Glacier National Park in the state of Washington, is Canada's arm of the International Peace Park. A ferry ride across the Straits of Georgia to Vancouver and the city of Victoria complete the transcontinental journey.

Trails in Canada

Canada has twenty-four National Parks and about as many regional parks. Each has always had its own network of trails but since 1970 hundreds of additional miles have been carved out.

One of the new trails is the Centennial Trail in British Columbia, which has been developed by students working on a grant from the federal government's Opportunities for Youth Program. The Centennial Trail stretches from the Simon Fraser University Campus in Vancouver to Manning Provincial Park 130 miles away. Much of it traverses scenic valleys, but in its approach to Manning Park it climbs to over 5,000 feet. Enroute there's historic Fort Langley, once a colonial outpost used by fur traders.

Some stretches of the Centennial Trail require the company of an experienced hiker, advises the Canadian Government Travel Bureau, but much of it can be enjoyed by the novice. Students marked the trail, widened it, built its bridges, laid log sections in corduroy fashion through swampy area and erected retaining walls to halt embankment erosion.

Because much of the trail lies nearby the Trans Canada Highway, sections can be used for afternoon or weekend outings. Topographical maps of the areas covered by the Centennial Trail are available from the Queens Printer at the Parliament Buildings, Victoria, British Columbia.

To the north, the far north, where Canada's Yukon abuts Alaska in an area just north of Juneau, the United States and Canada in a joint effort have reopened thirty-five miles of the historic Chilkoot and White Pass Trail. Prospectors who packsacked their possessions over this route in 1898 called it "the worst trail this side of hell." It's not heavenlike yet, but overnight cabins at strategic points along the way help make it a much easier journey.

The newly-completed Rideau Trail in Ontario is already beginning to rival the famous Bruce Trail (see above) in popularity. Linking Ottawa with Kingston, the Rideau Trail winds 180 miles through country rich in lakes, forests, streams and a wide range of plant life. There are also several old mica and spatite mines along the route. Side trails are being added and permanent camp sites developed.

The Trail is maintained by the Rideau Trail Association (Box

2111, Station D, Ottawa). The club also organizes outings and provides background information and maps with each $2 student membership.

The Laurentide Trail, 120 miles in length, links the hill trails of Ottawa's popular Gatineau Park with the rolling Laurentian Mountains, north of Montreal. Canada's Highway 8 affords easy access to the trail for short hikes. The Canadian Youth Hostel Association (270 Maclaren St., Ottawa, or 1324 Sherbrooke W., Montreal, Quebec) has available trail maps.

During the summer of 1971, more than one hundred miles of trails in Mont Temblant Provincial Park in the Laurentians, and 250 miles of trails from Shawbridge to Ste. Agathe, also in the Laurentians, were cleared, mapped and marked through funds provided by the Opportunities for Youth Program. Coupled with existing trails, the vast network represents one of the most comprehensive hiking systems in Canada. It is easy to reach from northeastern United States.

The trails wander through forests to scenic outlooks, around lakes and past abandoned huts. Most of the trails lie within ten minutes of the Laurentian Autoroute and Laurentian Route 11, making the many towns and villages along the way convenient jumping-off points and centers for accommodations and food. Maps of the Laurentian trails are available from the Laurentian Ski Zone (300 Place d'Youville, Montreal, Quebec) at $1.50.

You can obtain additional information about hiking and camping in Canada from many sources. The Canadian Youth Hostel's Association (1406 West Broadway, Vancouver, B.C.) and the Alpine Club of Canada (2974 West 28th Ave., Vancouver, B.C.), which is comparable to the Sierra Club, will be helpful. The park warden in the area in which you're interested is another good source. For general information about an area, contact the Canadian Government Travel Bureau at one of its provincial offices or at Bureau Headquarters (150 Kent St., Ottawa). The bureau maintains free counseling services in many American cities, including the following:

Boston, Mass. 02199
263 Plaza
The Prudential Center

Chicago, Ill. 60602
100 North La Salle St.

Cincinnati, Ohio 45202
Room 1010
Enquirer Building
617 Vine Street

Cleveland, Ohio 44115
Winous-Point Building
1250 Euclid Ave.

Detroit, Mich. 48226
Book Building
1257–1259 Washington Blvd.

Los Angeles, Calif. 90014
510 West 6th St.

Minneapolis, Minn. 55402
124 South 7th St.
Northstar Center

New York, N.Y. 10019
680 Fifth Ave

Philadelphia, Penna. 19102
Suite 305
Three Penn Center

Pittsburgh, Penna. 15222
1001–1003 Jenkins Arcade
Liberty and Fifth Aves.

Rochester, N.Y. 14604
247 Midtown Pl.

San Francisco, Calif. 94104
600 Market St., Suite 2300
Crocker Plaza

Seattle, Wash. 98101
Suite 1117
Plaza 600
600 Stewart St.

Washington, D.C. 22036
N.A.B. Building
1771 N. Street N.W.

Appendix

Hiking and Camping Organizations

These are the principal organizations that promote backpacking. Those marked with an asterisk (*) are regional or national organizations with chapters or affiliated branches in many or all states, or, in the case of Canada, provinces:

American Walkers Association
6221 Robinson Rd.
Cincinnati, Ohio

American Youth Hostels*
20 West 17th St.
New York, N.Y. 10011

The Appalachian Trail Conference*
1718 N St., N.W.
Washington, D.C. 20036

California Alpine Club
244 Pacific Bldg.
San Francisco, Calif. 94103

The Federation of Western Outdoor Clubs*
201 S. Ashdale St.
West Covina, Calif. 91790

Florida Trail Association
33 S.W. 18th Terrace
Miami, Florida 33129

The Green Mountain Club
108 Merchants Row
Rutland, Vt. 05701

Keystone Trails Association
Box 144
Concordville, Penna.

Mazamas
909 N.W. 19th Ave.
Portland, Ore. 97209

The Mountaineers
Box 122
Seattle, Wash. 98111

National Audubon Society*
1130 Fifth Ave.
New York, N.Y. 10028

National Campers & Hikers
Association*
7172 Transit Rd.
Buffalo, New York 14221

The New England Trail Conference*
P.O. Box 153
Ashfield, Mass. 01330

The New York & New Jersey
Trail Conference*
G.P.O. Box 2250
New York, N.Y. 10001

Omaha Walking Club
5238 S. 22nd St.
Omaha, Neb. 68107

Pacific Crest Trail Conference
Hotel Green
50 Green St.
Pasadena, Calif.

The Ptarmigans
Box 1821
Vancouver, Wash. 98663

The Sierra Club*
1050 Mills Tower
270 Bush St.
San Francisco, Calif. 94104

Smoky Mountains Hiking
Club
201 South Purdue
Oak Ridge, Tenn.

Canada

The Alpine Club of Canada*
2974 West 28th Ave.
Vancouver 8, B.C.

Bruce Trail Association
33 Hardale Crescent
Hamilton, Ontario

Canadian Youth Hostels Association*
1407 West Broadway
Vancouver 9, B.C.

Niagara Escarpment Trail
Council
P.O. Box 1
St. Catherines, Ontario

Skyline Trail Hikers of the
Canadian Rockies
622 Madison Ave. S.W.
Calgary, Alberta

Toronto Hiking and Conservation Club
Box 121
Postal Station F
Toronto 5

Equipment Retailers and Manufacturers

Frames, packs, tents, sleeping bags, etc.

Note: An asterisk (*) indicates that a firm also manufactures certain equipment items.

CALIFORNIA

Berkeley
Sierra Designs*
4th and Addison Sts.
94710

The Ski Hut*
1615 University Ave.
94703

Glendale
Kelty Pack Inc.*
1807 Victory Blvd.
Box 3453
91201

La Canada
Sport Chalet
951 Foothill Blvd.
Box 626
91011

Monterey
Himalayan Industries*
807 Cannery Row
Box 950
93940

Riverside
Highland Outfitters
Box 121
92502

San Francisco
Abercrombie & Fitch
220 Post St.
94108

Gerry Mountain Sports*
228 Grant Ave.
94108

The Smilie Co.
536 Mission St.
94105

Ward
Gerry Mountaineering
   Equipment
80481

COLORADO

Boulder
Alp Sport
3245 Prairie Ave.
Box 1081
80302

Gerry Mountaineer Equip-
   ment*
Box 910
80302

Holubar Mountaineering*
1975 30th St.
80302

Colorado Springs
Survival Research
   Laboratories
17 Marland Road
80906

Denver
Ace Sporting Goods
5300 West 44th Ave.
80216

Colorado Outdoor Sports
  Corporation*
Box 5544
80217

Sports International
5042 East Hampden Ave.

World of Leisure
9th St. & Broadway

CONNECTICUT

Rockville
Blonstein's Camping Center
Route 83
Box 87
06066

GEORGIA

Atlanta
Georgia Outdoors
1945 Candler Rd.
30030

ILLINOIS

Chicago
Abercrombie & Fitch
9 North Wabash Ave.
60602

Bailey's Camping Equipment
25 West Van Buren

Camper's Center
8900 Waukegan Rd.

Chicago Camping Co.
5430 N. Clark

Todd's
5 South Wabash Ave.
60603

Evanston
Campfitters Ltd.
924 Davis

Lyons
Camper's Center
7215 Ogden Ave.

Maywood
Easy Camping
510 South Wood

MAINE

Freeport
L. L. Bean*
04032

MARYLAND

Baltimore
H & H Surplus Center
1104 West Baltimore St.
21223

Lee's Outdoors
2900 Indiana St.

Bethesda
Bishop's Ultimate Outdoor
  Equipment
6804 Millwood Road
20034

MASSACHUSETTS

Amherst
Eastern Mountain Sports
Route 9

Boston
Eastern Mountain Sports, Inc.
1041 Commonwealth Ave.
02215

Brighton
The Outdoorsman
117 Brighton Ave.

Cambridge
Climbers' Corner
55 River St.
02139

Cohasset
Stow-A-Way Products*
02025

Springfield
Climbers and Campers
510 Main St.
01105

Stoughton
Corcoran, Inc.
02072

Wellesley
Eastern Mountain Sports
189 Linden St.

Woburn
Climbers' Corner
48 Henshaw St.
01801

MICHIGAN

Detroit
Camporee
18300 Mt. Elliott

Farmington
Raupp Campfitters
288859 Orchard Lake Rd.

MINNESOTA

St. Paul
Gokey Co.
94 East 4th St.
55101

Waseca
Herter's Inc.
56093

NEW HAMPSHIRE

Intervale
Peter Limmer and Sons
03845

NEW JERSEY

Ramsey
Recreation Unlimited
926 Route 17

NEW MEXICO

Roswell
Army and Navy Surplus
88201

NEW YORK

Albany
Mountaineering Recreation
269 Central Ave.
12206

Binghamton
Eureka Camping Center
625 Conklin Rd.
13902

Latham
Mountaineering Recreation
960-A Troy Schenectady Rd.
12110

New York
Abercrombie & Fitch
Madison Ave. at 45th St.
10017

Camp and Trail Outfitters*
21 Park Place
10007

Kreeger & Son
30 West 46th St.
10036

Paragon Sporting Goods
367 Broadway
10010

Ogdensburg
Thomas Black & Sons
13669

Scarsdale
Alpine Recreation
455 Central Park Ave.
10583

NORTH CAROLINA

Highlands
Trailblazer
P.O. Box 1
28741

OREGON

Portland
Norm Thompson
1815 N.W. Thurman
97209

Oregon City
Larry's Sport Center
Oregon City Shopping Center

Gresham
Larry's Shopping Center
East Burnside & Main Sts.

PENNSYLVANIA

Mechanicsburg
Camping and Outdoor Equip-
    ment
Carlisle Pike
Route 11 (Rd No. 1)

Philadelphia
I. Goldberg
925 Walnut St.

UTAH

Salt Lake City
The Mountaineer
207 South 13th St. East
Timberline Sports, Inc.
2959 Highland Drive

WASHINGTON

Seattle
Alpine Hut
4725-30th Ave. N.E.
98105

Eddie Bauer Expedition
    Outfitter
1926 Third St.

Recreational Equipment Inc.
523 Pike St.
98108

Seattle Tent and Fabric
    Products Company
900 N. 137th Street
98133

WISCONSIN

Milwaukee
Laacke & Joys Co.
1433 North Water St.
53202

CANADA

ONTARIO

Ottawa
Thomas Black and Sons*
225 Strathcona Ave.

Lightweight Foods for Backpackers

CALIFORNIA

Bernard Food Industries
Box 487
St. James Park Station
222 S. 24th St.
San Jose 95103

Dri-Lite Foods
11333 Atlantic Ave.
Lynwood 90262

E-Z Food Products
1420 S. Western Ave.
Gardena

Richmoor Corp.
Box 2728
Van Nuys 91404

Trailwise Products
c/o Ski Hut
1615 University Ave.
Berkeley 94703

Trail Chef Foods
Box 60041
Terminal Annex
Los Angeles 90060

MASSACHUSETTS

Chuck Wagon Foods
Micro Drive
Woburn, Mass. 01801

Stow-A-Way Products
103 Ripley Rd.
Cohasset 02025

OHIO

National Packaged Trail Foods
(Seidel's Trail Packets)
632 East 185th St.
Cleveland 44119

OREGON

Oregon Freeze Dry Foods, Inc.
P.O. Box 666
Albany 97321

Hiking and Camping Information. State Agencies

ALABAMA

Dept. of Conservation
State Capitol
Montgomery 36104

Bureau of Publicity &
Information
State Capitol
Montgomery 36104

ALASKA

Dept. of Economic Development & Planning
Alaska Travel Division
Box 2391
Juneau 99801

ARIZONA

Arizona Development Board
1500 W. Jefferson St.
Phoenix 85007

ARKANSAS

Arkansas Publicity & Parks Commission
Room 412
State Capitol
Little Rock 72201

CALIFORNIA

Dept. of Parks & Recreation
Division of Beaches & Parks
P.O. Box 2390
Sacramento 95811

COLORADO

Dept. of Public Relations
State Capitol
Denver 80203

CONNECTICUT

State Park & Forest Commission
Hartford 06115

Connecticut Development Commission
State Office Bldg.
Hartford 06115

DELAWARE

State Park Commission
3300 Faulkland Rd.,
Wilmington 19808

Delaware State Development
Tourism Division
45 The Green
Dover 19901

DISTRICT OF COLUMBIA

National Capitol Region
National Park Service
1100 Ohio Drive S.W.,
Washington 20242

FLORIDA

Florida Park Service
101 West Gaines St.
Tallahassee

GEORGIA

Georgia Dept. of State Parks
7 Hunter St. S.W.
Atlanta 30334

HAWAII

Hawaii Visitors Bureau
2051 Kalakaua Ave.
Honolulu

IDAHO

Dept. of Commerce & Development
State House
Boise

ILLINOIS

Dept. of Conservation
Division of Parks & Memorials
100 State Office Building
Springfield 62706

INDIANA

Division of State Parks
Dept. of Conservation
616 State Office Bldg.

Indianapolis 46209
Indiana Tourist Assistance
  Council
State House
Indianapolis 46204

IOWA

Public Relations
State Conservation Commis-
  sion
East 7th & Court
Des Moines 50309

KANSAS

Dept. of Economic Develop-
  ment
State Office Bldg.
Topeka 66612

LOUISIANA

State Parks & Recreation
  Commission
Old State Capitol Bldg.
P.O. Drawer 1111
Baton Rouge 70821

MAINE

State Park & Recreation
  Commission
State House
Augusta 04330

Dept. of Economics Develop-
  ment
State House
Augusta

MARYLAND

Dept. of Forests & Parks
State Office Bldg.
Annapolis 21404

Tourist Divisions, Dept. of
  Economic Development
State Office Bldg.
Annapolis

MASSACHUSETTS

Dept. of Natural Resources
Ashburton Place
Boston

Massachusetts Dept. of
  Commerce
150 Causeway St.
Boston

MICHIGAN

Michigan Tourist Council
Stevens T. Mason Bldg.,
Lansing 48926

MINNESOTA

Division of State Parks
320 Centennial Office Bldg.
St. Paul 55101

MISSISSIPPI

Mississippi Park System
1104 Woolfolk Bldg.
Jackson

MISSOURI

Missouri State Park Board
P.O. Box 176
Jefferson City 65102

Division of Commerce &
   Industrial Development
Travel-Recreation Section
Jefferson Bldg.
Jefferson City

MONTANA

Advertising Dept., Montana
   Highway Commission
Helena 59601

NEBRASKA

Nebraskaland
State Capitol
Lincoln 68509

NEVADA

State Park System
Carson City 89701
Dept. of Economic Develop-
   ment
Carson City

NEW HAMPSHIRE

Division of Economic
   Development
State House Annex
Concord 03301

NEW JERSEY

Dept. of Conservation & Economics Development, Forests & Parks Section
P.O. Box 1889
Trenton 08625

Dept. of Conservation & Eco-
   nomic Development
State Promotion Section
P.O. Box 1889
Trenton

NEW MEXICO

State Tourist Division
302 Galisteo
Santa Fe 87501

State Park & Recreation
   Commission
P.O. Box 1147
Santa Fe

NEW YORK

Conservation Dept., Division
   of Lands & Forests, Bureau
   of Forest Recreation
State Campus
Albany 12226

Division of Parks, State Campus Site
Albany

Dept. of Commerce, Travel
   Bureau
112 State St.
Albany 12207

NORTH CAROLINA

Travel Information Division, Dept. of Conservation and Development
Raleigh 27602

NORTH DAKOTA

Travel Dept.
North Dakota State Capitol
Bismarck 58501

OHIO

Division of Parks & Recreation, Ohio Dept. of Natural Resources
1500 Dublin Rd.
Columbus 43212

Development Dept. Information Central
Room 1007
Ohio Depts. Bldg.
Columbus 43215

OKLAHOMA

Planning & Resources Board, Tourist Division
Will Rogers Memorial Bldg.
Room 500
Oklahoma City 73105

OREGON

Travel Information Division, State Highway Dept.
Salem 97310

PENNSYLVANIA

State Dept. of Forests & Waters
Harrisburg 17120

Travel Development Bureau, Dept. of Commerce
405 South Office Bldg.
Harrisburg

RHODE ISLAND

Division of Parks & Recreation
100 N. Main St.
Providence 02903

SOUTH CAROLINA

Division of State Parks, Commission of Forestry
P.O. Box 357
Columbia 29202

State Development Board
P.O. Box 927
Columbia 29202

SOUTH DAKOTA

Publicity Division, Dept. of Highways
Pierre 57501

TENNESSEE

Division of State Parks
235 Cordell Hull Bldg.
Nashville 3

Division of Information & Tourist Promotion
264 Cordell Hull Bldg.
Nashville

TEXAS

Parks & Wildlife Dept.
John H. Reagan Bldg.
Austin 78701

Texas Highway Dept. Travel &
   Information Division
Austin 78701

UTAH

Tourist & Publicity Council
Council Hall-State Capitol
Salt Lake City 84114

VERMONT

Dept. of Forests & Parks
Montpelier

VIRGINIA

Division of Parks
Suite 403
Southern States Bldg.
7th & Main Sts.
Richmond 23219

Division of Public Relations
   and Advertising
State Office Bldg.
Richmond 23219

WASHINGTON

Tourists Promotion Division,
   Dept. of Commerce and
   Economic Development
General Administration Bldg.
Olympia 98502

WEST VIRGINIA

Division of Parks & Recreation, Dept. of Natural
   Resources
State Office Bldg.
25305

Dept. of Commerce, Travel
   Development Division
State Capitol Bldg.
Charleston 25305

WISCONSIN

Vacation & Travel Service,
   Conservation Dept.
P.O. Box 450
Madison 53701

WYOMING

Travel Commission
2320 Capitol Ave.
Cheyenne 82001

Sierra Club, Local Chapters

(See page 138 for address of national headquarters)

ALASKA

Alaska Chapter
P.O. Box 2025
Anchorage 99501

ARIZONA

Grand Canyon Chapter
2950 North 7th Street
Phoenix 85014

CALIFORNIA

Kern-Kaweah Chapter
P.O. Box 3295
Bakersfield 93305

Ventana Chapter
P.O. Box 5667
Carmel 93921

Tehipite Chapter
P.O. Box 5396
Fresno 93755

Angles Chapter
2410 Beverly Blvd.
Los Angeles 90057

Loma Prieta Chapter
190 California Avenue
Palo Alto 94306

San Gorgonio Chapter
P.O. Box 1023
Riverside 92502

Mother Lode Chapter
P.O. Box 1335
Sacramento 95806

San Diego Chapter
P.O. 525
San Diego 92112

San Francisco Bay Chapter
1082 Mills Tower
220 Bush Street
San Francisco 94104

Santa Lucia Chapter
c/o Rible
1356 Avalon Street
San Luis Obispo 93401

Redwood Chapter
7233 Fir Crest Road
Sebastopol 95472

COLORADO

Rocky Mountain Chapter
P.O. Box 6312
Denver 80206

DISTRICT OF COLUMBIA

Potomac Chapter
235 Massachusetts Avenue NE
Washington 20002

FLORIDA

Florida Chapter
4885 Waterwitch Point Road
Orlando 32806

GEORGIA

Chattahoochee Chapter
4310 Northside Drive NW
Atlanta 30372

HAWAII

Hawaii Chapter
P.O. Box 5049
Honolulu 96814

KENTUCKY

Cumberland Chapter
Cave Spring Farm
Route 1
Nicholasville 40356

IDAHO

Northern Rockies Chapter
P.O. Box 1032
Salmon 83467

ILLINOIS

Great Lakes Chapter
616 Delles
Wheaton 60187

IOWA

Iowa Chapter
c/o Ladin
4235 Foster Drive
Des Moines 50312

LOUISIANA

Delta Chapter
465 Audubon Street
New Orleans 70118

MASSACHUSETTS

New England Chapter
P.O. Box 32
West Somerville
02144

MICHIGAN

Mackinac Chapter
409 Seymour Street
Lansing 48933

MINNESOTA

North Star Chapter
P.O. Box 80004
St. Paul 55108

MISSOURI

Ozark Chapter
P.O. Box 12424
Olivette 63122

NEVADA

Toiyabe Chapter
P.O. Box 677
Reno 89504

NEW   MEXICO

Rio Grande Chapter
P.O. Box 351
Los Alamos 87544

NEW YORK

Atlantic Chapter
250 West 57th Street
New York 10019

OHIO

Ohio Chapter
9791 Wildbrook Lane
Cincinnati 45231

OKLAHOMA

Oklahoma Chapter
c/o Person
4101 Wood Drive
Oklahoma City 73111

SOUTH CAROLINA

Joseph Le Conté Chapter
P.O. Box 463
Clemson 29631

WASHINGTON

Pacific Northwest
4534½ University Way NE
Seattle 98105

WISCONSIN

John Muir Chapter
14660 Golf Parkway
Brookfield 53005

TEXAS

Lone Star Chapter
27190 Lana Lane
Conroe 77301

UTAH

Uinta Chapter
P.O. Box 8393
Foothill Station
Salt Lake City 84108

CANADA

BRITISH COLUMBIA

Brittish Columbia Chapter
814 20th Street
West Vancouver

ONTARIO

Ontario Chapter
c/o Lind
50 Rathnelly Avenue
Toronto, 7

For Additional Reading:

BOOKS

Colby, C. B. and Angier, Bradford. *The Art and Science of Taking to the Woods*. New York: Collier Books, 1971. ($3.95)
Subtitled, "A Complete Encyclopedia of Outdoor Living." This 288-page volume comes close to being just that. It appraises various types of equipment and explains basic skills and advanced techniques for wilderness camping. Line drawings illustrate. The authors boast a century of experience in woods lore and craft.

Fletcher, Colin. *The Complete Walker*. New York: Alfred A. Knopf, 1971. ($7.95)
Now in its ninth printing, this book has become to backpacking what Charles Chapman's *Piloting, Seamanship and Small Boat Handling* is to boating and sailing. *The Whole Earth Catalog* said of it: "It will make you laugh out loud all the way through . . . Most important, though, it's the only backpacking book I've ever seen which . . . will actually tell you how to do it in great enough detail to enable you to just go out and do it."

Groene, Janet. *Cooking on the Go*. New York: Grosset & Dunlap, 1971. (5.95)
The cookbook for cruising sailors and wilderness campers who travel without refrigeration, without ovens, with one- or two-burner stoves on short water rations.

Jaeger, Ellsworth. *Wildwood Wisdom*. New York: The Macmillan Co., 1971. ($6.95)
An all-inclusive and very knowledgeable handbook covering everything from weekend fishing trips to wilderness vacations.

Janes, E. C. *Nelson's Encyclopedia of Camping*. New York: Thomas Nelson & Co., 1963. ($7.50)
Covers everything from angling and axes to vandalism and the weather, but is more suited for the family camper than the outdoorsman.

Merrill, W. K. *All About Camping*. Harrisburg, Penna: The Stackpole Co., 1963. ($4.95)
This handy reference volume is valuable for the descriptive information it gives concerning National Parks and Forests. Mr. Merrill is a retired National Park ranger.

Merrill, W. K. *The Hikers and Backpackers Handbook*. New York: Winchester Press, 1971. ($5.95)
"Just everything," says the publisher," including such subjects as desert camping and pack trains."

Ormand, Clyde. *Outdoorsman's Handbook*. New York: E. P. Dutton, 1970. ($5.95)
Practical tips and techniques on becoming a skilled woodsman.

Sussman, Aaron and Goode, Ruth. *The Magic of Walking*. New York: Simon and Schuster, 1967. ($7.50)
A big book — 410 pages — with chapters such as "The Rediscovery of Walking," "Why Walking is Good Medicine," "A Beginners Recipe for Walking," and "The Science and Art of Walking," this has to rank as the definitive piece of writing on the subject.

GOVERNMENT PUBLICATIONS

Publications prepared by the U.S. Department of the Interior and available from the Superintendent of Documents (U.S. Government Printing Office, Washington, D.C. 20402) include the following:

The Appalachian Trail, 5¢; a map, safety suggestions and brief descriptions of points of interest.

Back-Country Travel in the National Park System, 35¢; a forty-page booklet describing individual parks.

Boating Regulations in the National Park System, 30¢

Camping in the National Park System, 25¢; an eighteen-page booklet contains general information and descriptive material concerning camping accommodations in the National Parks.

Fishing in the National Park System, 30¢

National Forest Wilderness and Primitive Areas, 15¢; a twelve-page booklet giving information on the origin, development and management of wilderness and primitive areas.

National Parks of the United States, $1.50; a packet of maps and folders.

Outdoor Recreation in the National Forests, 60¢; a broad view of the recreational activities and opportunities in the National Forests; 106 pages, illustrated.

Wilderness, 20¢; a description of the wild and primitive lands of the wilderness areas maintained by the National Forest System; sixteen pages, illustrated.

TRAIL GUIDES

Adirondack Canoe Routes, William G. Howard, State of New York Conservation Department, Albany, New York.

Bruce Trail Guide Book, Bruce Trail Association, 33 Hardale Crescent, Hamilton, Ontario, Canada.

Canoeing — Camping in the Boundary Waters Canoe Area, U.S. Forest Service, Federal Building, Duluth, Minnesota 55801.

Circuit Hikes in the Shenandoah National Park, George Huber, Ed. Potomac Appalachian Trail Club, Washington, D.C.

Cascade Crest Trail Washington, *Pacific Crest Trail System*, Forest Service, U.S. Department of Agriculture, Pacific Northwest Region, Portland, Oregon 96208.

Catskill Trails, W. D. Mulholland, State of New York Conservation Department, Albany, N.Y.

Connecticut Walk Book, Publication No. 361, Connecticut Forest and Park Association, Inc., Hartford, Connecticut.

Guide to Adirondack Trails, High Peak Region and Northville-Placid Trail. The Adirondack Mountain Club, Inc., Gabriels, Franklin County, New York.

Guide to the Appalachian Trail. The Appalachian Trail Conference, Inc., 1718 "N" Street, N.W., Washington, D.C. 20036.

A Guide to Climbs and Hikes in Midwestern Oregon, Jim Wagner, Ed. Oregon State University Mountain Club, Corvallis, Oregon.

Guide to the Horse-Shoe Trail in Pennsylvania, Horse-Shoe Trail Club, Inc., 1600 Three Penn Center Plaza, Philadelphia, Pa.

The Long Trail, Green Mountain Club, Inc., 108 Merchants Row, Rutland, Vermont.

Roads and Trails of Olympic National Park, Frederick Leissler, University of Washington Press, Seattle, Washington.

Pacific Crest Trails, Joseph T. Hazard. Superior Publishing Company, Seattle, Washington.

Pennsylvania Hiking Trails, Keystone Trails Association, Box 144, Concordville, Pennsylvania.

Rocky Mountain National Park, Souvenir and Trail Guide, Timberline Trails Co., P.O. Box 757, Littleton, Colorado.

Rocky Mountain Trails, Timberline Trails Co., P.O. Box 757, Littleton, Colorado.

Routes and Rocks, Hiker's Guide to the North Cascades from Glacier Peak to Lake Chelan, D. F. Crowder and R. W. Tabor, The Mountaineers, Box 122, Seattle, Washington 98111.

Thirty Hikes in Alaska: Western Chugach, Talkeetna Kenai, by William E. Hauser, The Mountaineers, Box 122, Seattle, Washington, 98111.

Trail Guide to Sauaro National Monument, Eber Glendening. Southern Arizona Hiking Club, Box 12122, Tucson, Arizona.

Trails in the Lake George Region, NYS Conservation Department, Division of Lands and Forests, Albany, New York.

Trails to Marcy, A. S. Hopkins, State of New York Conservation Department, Albany, New York.

Trails in the Schroon Lake Region, State of New York Conservation Department, Bureau of Forest Recreation, Albany, New York.

Trips and Trails, E. M. Sterling. Published by The Mountaineers, Box 122, Seattle, Washington 98111.

Starr's Guide, Guide to the John Muir Trail and the High Sierra Region, Walter A. Starr, Jr., Sierra Club, 270 Bush St., San Francisco, California 94104.

Wilderness Boating on Yellowstone Lakes, John de la Montogue, Superintendent, Yellowstone National Park, Wyoming 83020.

Index

N

National Audubon Society, 7
The National Campers and Hikers
  Association, 7
National Forest, 117, 139, 140, 141,
  147
National Forest Service, 8, 139, 144,
  146
National Grasslands, 140
The National Park Regional offices,
  124, 125
National Park Rules and
  Regulations, 125
National Wilderness Preservation
  System, 140
New England Trail Conference, 4;
  publications, 4
New York State Department of
  Commerce, 116
New York–New Jersey Trail
  Conference, 4; publications, 4
North America, 7
North American Indians, 66
North Cascades National Park, 136
The North Country Trail, 123
North and South Absoroka
  Wilderness Area, 144
Northwest Territory, 153

O

Ocala National Forest, 141
Okanogan National Forest, 147
Oliver, James, 56
Olympic National Park, 136
Opportunities for Youth Program,
  155
Optimus, Inc., 81, 82, 84
Oregon Freeze Dry Foods, 58
Organ-Pipe Cactus National
  Monument, 136
Overnight camping, 96–114
Ovens: reflector, 90; Dutch oven, 90

P

The Pacific Coast Trail, 119
Pacific Northwest Cascades, 5
Pack, 11, 12; packing of, 41, 42
Pack animals, 5

Packbag, 13, 14, 15, 19; pockets, 41,
  42
Packframe, 11, 12, 13, 14, 15, 19, 40;
  size, 14; fabric, 15
Packframe backbands, 13
Packframe harness, 13, 19
Packframe versatility, 15
Packframe waistbelt, 13, 19
Pack weight, 19, 40, 41
Palisades Interstate Park, 116
Pants, 28
Parka: down-filled, 31; windproof,
  31; cost, 31
Personal Hygiene, 34
Personal hygiene items, 34
Personal medical needs, 38, 39
Physical demands, 3
Pisgah National Forest, 141
Point Reyes National Seashore, 136
Poncho, 29, 109
Provisions, 4

Q

Quadrangle maps, 8

R

Rain protection, 28, 29
Recipes, 91–94
Recreation gear, 36
Redwood National Park, 136
Rideau Trail, 154
Rideau Trail Association, 154, 155
Riding Mountain National Park, 153
Rocky Mountain National Park, 137
Rocky Mountain Region, 144
Rocky Mountains, 140, 143
Rope, 109, 110
Rucksack, 19

S

Saguaro National Monument, 137
Salt, 70
San Luis Peak, 144
San Pedro Parks Wilderness Area, 43
Sanitation, 56, 57
Santa Fe National Park, 143
Sawtooth Mountain, 5
Selkirk Mountain, 109
Selway-Bitterroot Area, 144